power
&
Poetry

power & Poetry

Best Practices for High School Classrooms

Jim Mahoney & **Jerry Matovcik**

Heinemann
Portsmouth, NH

Heinemann
A division of Reed Elsevier Inc.
361 Hanover Street
Portsmouth, NH 03801–3912
www.heinemann.com

Offices and agents throughout the world

Library of Congress Cataloging-in-Publication Data
Mahoney, Jim.
    Power and poetry : best practices for high school classrooms / Jim Mahoney and Jerry
Matovcik.
        p. cm.
    Includes bibliographical references and index.
    ISBN 0-325-00730-6 (acid-free paper)
    1. English language—Composition and exercises—Study and teaching (Secondary).
2. Poetry—Authorship—Study and teaching (Secondary). 3. Creative writing
(Secondary education).   I. Matovcik, Jerry.   II. Title.

LB1576.M358 2005
808'.042'0712—dc22   2005015346

Editor: James Strickland
Production: Vicki Kasabian
Cover design: Joni Doherty
Typesetter: Reuben Kantor, QEP Design
Manufacturing: Donata Luz, Louise Richardson

Printed in the United States of America on acid-free paper
09 08 07 06 05 DA 1 2 3 4 5

for

All of those students who trusted us and took writing risks,
sensing they had something to say,
creating beautiful words and works,

All of those teachers who attended our workshops
or visited our classrooms,
giving us encouragement,
urging us on,

and
for Jim Strickland,
who encouraged us to write our stories,
nudging us at the hard parts,
cheering us on.

Contents

Acknowledgments

From Jerry Matovcik

For my wife, Ronnie, who has made so many things possible in my teaching and in my life.

I am grateful to Jim Mahoney for his invitation to come along and clear the pasture spring.

To John Newcombe for listening with an attentive ear.

To Heather, Jay, Juliet, and Viola for their support and for all the poetry readings on Fire Island.

To Melissa, Tom, and Kenneth for their support, and for sunny afternoons full of Montauk daisies.

And to Jim Strickland, our benefactor, whose patience and encouragement made this book possible.

From Jim Mahoney

For Helen Sandiford, who dubbed me "Sportswriter" in seventh grade; Jerry Matovcik, who got me going again in poems, Whitman, and things; Brian Mahoney, who continues to surprise and please me with his poems, just as he is surprised and pleased with Finn, his baby son; WTP, who gives me good words and poems.

To Marguerite, my mother, a teacher herself, who gave me my first words. To Edward, my father, who unabashedly bellowed out songs and poems. To Eileen, my wife, who continues to give me space and who has encouraged every move I've made.

For Jennifer Abrams for her willingness to read the first chapters and to shout for more. For Kathleen Strickland, who also read the first efforts and saw something good, giving those chapters to her students who, in turn, gave me positive feedback and encouragement to continue the hard work of writing when it seemed easier to give it all up. For Vicki Kasabian, at Heinemann, who has produced this book with understanding and care.

Preface

Strange things happen during the course of writing a book. This text began in 2001 when Jim Strickland, editing *Power and Portfolios* (2002), suggested cutting out more than fifty pages devoted to poetry, saying that I should save these pages for the next book; not only was he convinced that I would write another book—it would be on teaching poetry. At the time, I was so overwhelmed with the first book that I swore there would never be a second book. But when *Power and Portfolios* finally arrived with its glossy cover and warm response, I remembered Jim's words, somehow forgetting about the pain of the writing process, and began to think of the poetry book and of all the text that I already had written and saved on a disk. I invited Jerry Matovcik to join me in writing this book, since he had so much to do with the practices and approaches we used in the classrooms mentioned in *Power and Portfolios*. We brainstormed, outlined chapters, divvied up areas, and began to write—he on Long Island and I in Yardley, Pennsylvania. We decided that we should each retain our own voice as we told our stories, by writing different chapters rather than writing each chapter together.

I have a great desire as a reader to hear the voice of the teacher–educator who is telling the story, and I think other readers have a similar feeling. So, while much of this story is told through my voice, Jerry is in my head throughout, guiding me, reminding me to add something, and providing me with explanations and information that I don't have. We worked side by side for ten years, in nearby classrooms and in countless workshops and staff development sessions, helping teachers to turn over some of the power to their students and showing the potential power of poetry when used properly in the classroom. During these times, Jerry was teaching me a great deal, and I was showing him a thing or two. I hope that when you hear my voice in many of the chapters, you also hear Jerry's, in his quiet, unassuming way. If this happens, you will have begun an exciting journey in using poetry to empower students and to enrich their lives and yours.

Prologue

The Mountain Whippoorwill

The scene appeared to be lifted right out of *To Kill a Mockingbird*. Brady stood in the front of a packed Mount Sinai Congregational Church, just as Atticus Finch did in the Maycomb County Court Room. Even the balcony was full as members of the congregation leaned forward to listen to a college boy tell his story in verse form. Recounting Stephen Vincent Benet's tale of how "Hill-Billy Jim won first prize in the Georgia Fiddlers' Contest," Brady told how he himself, a victim of cystic fibrosis since he was small, was overcoming similar odds against his disease. For over nine minutes, Brady dramatically presented Benet's long poem of the poor mountain boy who, with his fiddle named the Mountain Whippoorwill, overcame the odds to beat out a group of experienced fiddlers at the annual contest. The audience was mesmerized from the sad beginning when we learn that the boy doesn't have a mother, father, or even "a whole pair of pants," to the intimidating description of the other fiddlers, among them Old Dan Wheeling, "king-pin fiddler for nearly twenty years," to the rousing rhythm when Jim starts to play. At dawn, Jim finishes, thinking he is defeated, but instead receives thunderous applause and a hand of congratulation from Old Dan himself. It is a moving occasion for the congregation and they reward Brady with their own thunderous applause.

Sitting in the front row, clapping louder than the rest, was his teacher, Jerry Matovcik, who had been invited by Brady to this occasion. Four years earlier as a senior in high school, Brady learned the words and movements that he would recite in the days and years following. Brady's dramatic presentation had its origins years earlier when we watched storyteller and then English teacher, Marni Gillard, recite the Benet poem at a statewide conference on writing. On the following Monday morning, Jerry began to memorize the poem himself for our annual high school poetry reading to take place in two weeks. Each

1

day for about a week, during our free second period, Jerry would recite the poem to me, and I'd offer tips on delivery and gestures. The poetry reading would last all day, and teachers would bring their classes to attend during their English period. Jerry got up the courage to recite the poem during the first period reading. Brady, a junior, marginally passing, was in the audience at the time. On returning to the classroom, Brady asked for a copy of the poem. School let out for the summer and Brady moved on to his senior year.

In the fall, Brady enrolled in Jerry's senior elective writing/reading workshop course. Hearing the poem again in class, Brady approached him for help in learning it by heart. In a matter of weeks, Brady was delivering the poem to all of our classes and growing more forceful and confident with each performance. Each time, the students were amazed at and appreciative of his accomplishment.

In the months that followed, Brady found several occasions to recite the poem until he presented the poem at the schoolwide end-of-the-year poetry reading. His first period performance was so successful that he was invited to repeat it during later periods. Brady was not only hooked on performing this poem but had begun to identify with the young boy in the poem. When Brady went to college, he continued to perform the poem and he even began to sign his letters as "The Whippoorwill."

A letter from Brady the following year told of a semester break journey with a group of college students to Appalachia to help to build homes for those who needed them. Each night after the day's work was done, the students would gather around the campfire to sing, tell stories, and enjoy each other's company. Brady presented "The Mountain Whippoorwill" to the group and repeated it at the group's request. It seemed that the more Brady lived with and performed the poem, the more he was reaching out to others, working in programs to help the less fortunate, even reciting his poem at a church, with his teacher present. Today, Brady is married and teaches physical education at an elementary school in New York State. Who could ever have guessed the power that a poem would have on the lives of so many people, including The Whippoorwill himself?

1

The Power of Poetry—
Food for the Soul

The May sun beat down on the spectators in the stands, warming the dignitaries under the tent at the Walt Whitman Birthplace Association's annual poetry festival honoring the best student poets on Long Island. Each year, a well-known poet is invited to be present, to read from his or her works, and to honor the occasion of Walt Whitman's birthday. Poets such as William Stafford, Adrienne Rich, Galway Kinnell, Sharon Olds, and others have been there. On this particular Sunday, I stood at the podium under the tent and helped a senior deliver his poem. Jesse Yim, a student in my remedial twelfth-grade English class, had won first place for all eleventh and twelfth graders on Long Island. In "Two Oceans," a touching poem about looking backward and looking forward, Jesse told the story of how "The sun rises over the glossy Yellow Ocean at Po-Hang," an ocean he knew in his homeland of Korea just two years before, and how "The sun sets over the crimson Atlantic Ocean at Fire Island," the Atlantic Ocean that he had come to know when he came to America. Four younger first place winners had read and now it was his time. Because of his language barrier and difficulty speaking well, he had asked me to read his poem for him, but I finally convinced him to read it with me. When we finished, the audience broke into loud applause. Under the tent, sitting next to the podium was Allen Ginsburg, that year's featured poet. As we listened to the applause, Ginsburg turned and bowed to Jesse several times, according to the customs of Korea. Jesse bowed back and then smiled as they shook hands. It was a wonderful moment; the power of poetry had spoken.

Sadness and Wonderment

At a time when high-stakes testing has intimidated so many teachers and administrators into unending drilling for the tests, many students have been robbed of the opportunity to write and to find poetry that can produce the ranges of sadness and wonderment in their lives. They are deprived of the kind of opportunities that Jesse had to use poetry to express their deepest feelings about what matters to them. They are deprived of the food needed to sustain their souls, the bread of poetry.

Poetry is power. The central issue in most of our lives is the question of power. Someone always wants someone to do something or be someone. People have an inclination to want to control things. The question of power is at the heart of most schools—gaining control of a curriculum, or a faculty, or a department, getting control of a class or a student, or controlling policies. Generally left out of this equation are the very students themselves. They seem to have no power, no voice, no choice. Most decisions about how, when, and how much they will learn are by and large determined by someone else.

The Most Powerful Genre

And yet, poetry seems to be one of the most powerful genres around. It is often the one thing that students will attach themselves to, if given the proper attention. The memorials that sprang up immediately following the attack on the World Trade Center in September 2001 were not essays. Short stories, novels, and plays were not placed in places around Ground Zero. No, the one constant genre of expression, taking every form and shape, was poetry. It wasn't assigned and it wasn't graded, but it came. It was a rendering of the heart, the outward expression of the pain within. It didn't have to get a check mark or be handed in, but it found its way into public places. Poetry was the expression of people from all walks of life and all social stations. Some wrote their own while others used published poems. When we give students the opportunity to come to poetry, we are giving them a power that can vitalize a classroom and compose a life.

My former chairperson at Commack High School South, and later the man I would replace as he lay dying of cancer, had once written a poem that his good friend and English teacher, Jack McGrath, recited at Ed's funeral. This poem captures the power that poetry has.

Sadness and Wonderment
It is a sad and wondrous thing to be a poet.
It is always thistles of memory driving over
the fields of sleep, all the voices of childhood,
like moon phantoms chasing along the canyons of dream.
It is the pain of blue days in June,
when all the words fall away, like birds blown backward in the storm.
It is one bright leaf too many—
or the high cry of wild geese in a far wind.
It is all the lovely words that never let us go.
Who said, "The wild, old Atlantic is shouting on the sand"?
It is the other meanings in a mother's eyes
and yourself, apple green, dropping into tomorrow.
And finally, it is going one long walk around
the center of yourself, coming to the silent core
and knowing you are there.

—*Ed Leigh*

Poetry Units?

Giving students poetry is like feeding them nourishing food. I used to save my poetry units for the spring, somehow associating poetry with the flowers blooming, perhaps thinking of Wordsworth's daffodils swaying gently with the breeze. But I've come to feel sad for those students who have had poetry withheld for most of the year, only to have it trotted out at the end of the year when their energy is focused on the upcoming summer. Poetry isn't something like a Thanksgiving turkey that can be brought out for us to stuff ourselves for a short period of time. Poetry is food that we need in regular amounts so that we can stay healthy.

In time, I came to realize that writers need frequent exposure to reading poetry and ample opportunity to write it all year long. Poetry needs to be integrated with all of the work studied throughout the year, not compartmentalized into four short weeks of a unit. It shouldn't be a unit unto itself but should be part of each unit.

Of course, poetry is a legitimate genre, worthy of study, but it is much more. It is one of the best and most efficient ways for students to deal with the events of their lives. Georgia Heard (1999b) tells of a young boy named Casey, caught making off with a class copy of a poetry anthology by concealing it beneath his jacket. Heard suggested copying his favorite poem into his notebook rather than "borrowing" the class books. He copied Myra Cohn Livingston's "Help," a poem about a child praying her father would come home to the family but doubting that even prayer would be able to help. Heard concludes by saying,

> Casey had discovered that poetry could provide some understanding and company with the difficult emotions he was having and feeling so alone with. He and hundreds of other children are discovering the deep power, truth, and joy of poetry. Maybe that should be our goal: for all children to feel so connected to poetry that they too want to slip a poetry book into their jackets, to keep them company at home, and for all of their lives.

Poetry All Year Long

I don't spend the first day of school going over a million rules and requirements of the course as some do; instead, I like to get right into poetry, on a personal level, not analyzing it but connecting to it, immersing ourselves in it. I start the first day of school with two poems about going to school—"September, the First Day of School" by Howard Nemerov, and "Daughter Waiting for a School Bus" by Amon Grinnan. Both poems relate the feelings of parents for their children's experiences as they begin their first day at school or wait for the bus. On the sheet containing both poems, I ask students to respond by recalling their own very first day of school, or recording their feelings on the morning of the present day. I even give them the option to write it from their parents' point of view, imagining what they might have thought as they sent their child off to school. This way, they see poetry in action and how it helps make sense of their lives, dealing with the past and present.

Victor Jaccarino, an English department chairperson, asks prospective candidates how and why they would teach poetry. He hopes that they understand that poetry helps to nurture students by their writing poems and reading them. He hopes that a prospective teacher knows that poetry feeds first and then becomes a subject for study.

If Victor asked me his interview question, I would tell him of the time Louise Rosenblatt found a question following a poem in an anthology, "What fact does this poem teach?" Poems don't teach facts; poetry isn't a convenient text for short answer questions. I don't think that student literacy is improved or one's quality of life is enriched by such approaches to literature. I believe that students' love of reading and writing will grow by showing them how poetry can connect to their lives and act as a source of expression, and with it, their ability to do well on state tests.

Where Poems Hide

Georgia Heard (1999a) suggests that we all have poems hiding in and around us, and she asks where poetry hides for each of us. I ask my students this, too, and they write about it in their writer's notebooks. I answer the same question and show them my answer. This is where poetry hides for me.

Curing Inertia
Poems lie quietly for me in the clutter of the kitchen table,
in the quiet of a Sunday morning,
when a simple cup of coffee
will bring them out of hiding for only precious minutes.

They creep out, having been sealed up for too long,
getting little chance to breathe these days,
having no freedom to run and play for a while.

They have been put away,
like exercises of years ago,
the jogs and the tennis matches,
or the joys of shooting hoops alone for hours.

No more.
The body breaks down when not cared for
and so does the soul.
It takes an open pad, a ready pen

7

and a sliver of Sunday silence
to entice the soul to play with
a locked up poem,
even for ten minutes,
to cure inertia and
start the day.

—*Jim Mahoney*

Former poet laureate Robert Pinsky had a hunch that poetry was more popular with the American people than most thought. As part of his "Favorite Poem Project," he sent out college English students in the Washington, DC, area to ask visitors if they had a favorite poem and, when they usually did, if they would be willing to recite it into tape recorders that the students carried. Thousands submitted a favorite poem and explained why the poem was important to them. Pinsky felt the project was successful because each individual was free to choose a poem personally important. In addition, he believed that the recitation gives the poem a kind of completeness that occurs when it is finally delivered to the community.

It is our job to help students find out where poems hide for them and to bring them out. Perhaps some of the stories that Jerry and I tell in the pages that follow will provide some practical examples for teachers who wish to make a dramatic change in the diet and health of their students, empowering them to see their world in clearer ways than they've ever seen before.

Play in Teaching and Learning

Pullover
Lovable—

The elastic bands
clasp my wrists,
insulated warmth surrounding
my upper body.

Thermal—

Its soft touch caresses
my exhausted head
resting on my maroon sleeves.

Encompassing—

Pullover is always there for me,
whenever the temperature
falls below an acceptable number.

Versatile—

Covering my body,
sheltering me from the elements.

—Jeanine Beatty

In her reflection in her final portfolio, Jeanine wrote the following about how she and her friend, Kerri, worked side by side to write their poems:

In order to avoid Kerri murdering me, I need to lay it all out on the table.

Picture it. One day during English, we're sitting in the computer room. It was one of those days that was really cold and (since the school has hardly any heat in the winter) some people had their gloves with them. We sat at our computers, hunting for topics to write about. Kerri glanced at the worn black gloves that lay beside her computer and said, "I'm going to write a poem about my gloves!" I thought it was a good idea so I decided, since I couldn't think of anything else, to write a poem about my maroon pullover. So now you know that it was not my original idea. I copied Kerri.

Well, not exactly. Hers was a little different. In Kerri's poem, she takes different words describing her gloves and puts them in a list form. Besides, it's been done before: people write funny poems about topics similar to this all the time.

In writing "Pullover," I decided to use a unique approach by choosing one descriptive word about the pullover and explaining the positive characteristic in the following stanza. Also in this piece, I wrote directly onto the computer instead of using my Writer's Notebook—an unusual occurrence.

Anyway, I really like this poem because of its humorous nature. It tells you the truth; I really don't think that the poem itself is that bad. This piece differs from the rest of my writing because it isn't about anything serious and I wasn't trying to make it perfect. I was just trying to have fun.

Michael Smith and Jeff Wilhelm (2002) reiterate the theory of flow as articulated by psychologist Mihaly Csikszentmihalyi as "joy, creativity, the process of total involvement with life." This idea of flow comes from Csikszentmihalyi's study of what brings people happiness; it comes down to people being so involved in an activity that nothing else seems to matter. They lose all sense of time as they become fully absorbed in their activity. Flow has eight characteristics that Smith and Wilhelm have collapsed to four: "a sense of control and competence, a challenge that requires an appropriate level of skill, clear goals and feedback, and a focus on the immediate experience" (Smith and Wilhelm 2002, 30).

The way we have both structured and opened up avenues for our students' writing and learning, we have observed, that when they are engaged in poetry, there is this feeling of flow for them. Because poems are usually short, students get feedback and a sense of accomplishment faster and in a more satisfying way. Jeanine and Kerri were playing around, completely absorbed in creating at the computer, without any sense of evaluation hinging on their work. They were in the flow. As we describe some of the approaches we've taken in the following chapters, we hope to show how students play around in most of the things they write, giving them that sense of flow that Csikszentmihalyi has witnessed.

10

2

Writing Small

Every September, on a day when I saw that the weather was comfortable, I would take my students for a walk outside, notebooks in hand. I even had some clipboards with paper handy for those students who had either forgotten their notebook or who found a clipboard easier to work with. I would explain briefly that we would be stopping from time to time to write in precise detail all of the things they noticed, large or small. Then we headed for the far fence by the edge of the woods. But I would stop first as we neared the middle of the soccer field and I'd gather the students, telling them to sit on the grass, be perfectly quiet, and record all of the sights, sounds, and other sensory details they could. I pointed out things like newly mown grass, soccer cleat marks in the dirt, clumps of weeds, and insects crawling about. I also asked them to listen for sounds and movement in the school building we were leaving behind. They could look at the sky, stare off in the distance, imagine, and notice. As they did so, I told them they should record rapidly the things that struck them. If they had to talk to someone about the things they saw, they were to do so in whispers.

After five minutes, we made our way past the far side of the soccer field, just inside the fence. Again, we stopped to look back at the school for a longer perspective, even noticing things on the roof, such as an antenna, various wires, rust dripping from the tan bricks. They could further record sights from the ground they were standing or sitting on, or turn their attention to the mannerisms of their classmates.

Finally, we would walk through the passageway in the fence and walk along the beaten path in the woods, stopping to notice fallen trees, spider webs, nests, and other aspects of the area. With about twenty-five minutes gone in the period, I would tell students that we would be heading back to the classroom where we would spend the rest of the period going over the things recorded, filling in details, adding texture and hue, and then talking about what we noticed. Though many students listed things that others had recorded, all students seemed to have something that no other person had or that no one else had seen in quite the same way, including me. I read some of my observations as well and then I showed them how I made some comparisons using a simile or a metaphor. I looked at the crack in the brick of the building and compared it to a split in the side of a battleship. The bare spot in front of the goal on the soccer field became a sink hole, and the fence was a rusty barrier. Students added some of their own figurative language to their notes. They had the option of developing these notes further, turning them into a poem or a prose piece, or simply using the class as an activity in noticing and recording.

Students always took this experience seriously with little fooling around. They knew they were being given an opportunity to look at ordinary sights and sounds and to see them in ways they had not noticed before. The words we used again and again for this kind of recording was *writing small,* a term from Ralph Fletcher's *A Writer's Notebook* (1996). By this expression, students came to know that there was much going on around them that they often took for granted and by slowing down their lives and taking note of each aspect, they could see life more fully in all its details.

I would often repeat this walk in the middle of winter, perhaps in late February or early March, when some snow was still on the ground but starting to melt, yet not enough to hinder us from a short walk. Students would stop at the same places they had observed in September and would record things they noticed, such as the crystals of melting ice, the patches of grass emerging from the receding snow, even the leafless trees, swaying in the winter winds. If the weather was too severe, I would have them view the outside from the inside, noticing the everyday things in a new light.

John, a twelfth grader in a "skills" class, won a prize in the Walt Whitman Poetry Contest for his poem about a walk we made in the snow.

Peace

Walking across the soccer field
on the short, green grass,
occasionally walking thorough a patch of snow
and listening to the sound of it
as it packs underfoot.

On through the forest,
over the fallen trees and limbs,
leaves crunching while I walk the forest floor,
as the wind whips through the branches above,
where the crows stop to nest.

Finally, a field that seems almost endless,
as the brisk wind whistles through the tall yellow weeds,
and blows across my face, leaving my cheeks cold and red.
There seemed to be a big shadow of a cloud on the field,
only there were no clouds.
In the distance, there are cars driving
past the peaceful little red barn on 25A.

As I sit here on this old rusted barrel,
in the middle of this wheat field,
I can't help but wish that the world I left behind me
was as peaceful as this.

—John Rodecker

Jen, an eleventh grader, looked out the classroom window to the same scene that John had walked through the period before and she wrote the following poem.

Picture Window

Tree upon tree,
Brown and leafless,
Chain-linked fence,
Cold and silver,
On an empty field.
Hard metal bench,
For unused players.
Snow-covered ground,

Few brown spots.
Bright sun reflection.
I squint my eyes.

—*Jen Manttari*

The purpose of this activity was to give students practice in observing, of slowing life down and becoming aware of the life around them. Lucy Calkins (1992) referred to this as leading "wide-awake lives," sensing things going on around them that they were often in too much of a rush to notice. When we allow students to write small, they learn how to notice the important details of their lives and to record them for themselves.

From the first day of class, I ask students to bring their writer's notebook home and to spend a few minutes observing and writing just as they have done in class, and to bring those notebooks back to class each day. I am encouraging them to take their writer's notebook beyond the walls of the classroom and to use it to record the wide-awake moments of their life, to do what real writers do.

3

The Writer's Notebook

I used to believe in the use of a journal to help with students' writing
fluency but I think I "journaled" them to death. I required one entry a
week, sometimes on topics I assigned but mostly of their own choice,
usually done outside of class. Typically, the evening before the journals
were due at the end of each quarter, there would be a flurry of writing
activity by students. I put so much time into responding to each student's journal and the students put a good amount of effort in writing
these entries, even if they were done at the last minute. None of this
writing, however, was ever developed further. Instead, it only served to
satisfy my journal writing assignments. I thought of it later as empty
writing, done for me, going nowhere, except for a grade.

But then Jerry and I learned about using a writer's notebook from
Donald Graves in 1989 at a Dowling College conference. During his
talk, Graves read from his writer's notebook and challenged us to get
our own and write for ten minutes each day. That very afternoon, on
my way home, I bought myself such a notebook and I wrote on the
cover Graves' challenge: "Write for ten minutes a day, no rewrites, just
record the things that are on your mind." As I began to write regularly
in my notebook, I saw that it might have value for my students. I had
a hunch that this sort of a notebook could be a place where they could
write regularly and begin to pile up little things that they could turn
into finished pieces, including poems and other literary forms.

A writer's notebook is equally important for writing poetry. My current
writer's notebook is called *Birch Seedlings and Birch Trimmings* because of
my long-time admiration of Robert Frost and my portfolio called *A
Swinger of Birches*. I love the speaker's philosophy in Frost's "Birches"
because he expresses a way of living to which I aspire. The speaker loves
to climb his father's trees, and even dreams of escaping to another world

by climbing a snow-white birch trunk till the tree couldn't hold his weight anymore and dips him, down again. He knows that this is all just weariness and a temporary thought. He says that our lives on earth are the proper place for love. This seems to me to be the mission of a teacher; the classroom allows for teachers to connect with students. A writer's notebook is a place for such nurturing. I share some of the things I've written in my writer's notebook, even photocopying a page and making a transparency of it to show students the stages of my work.

Writing Small

I ask students to "write small," as Ralph Fletcher suggests, to record a moment in their life, to capture in precise detail something they notice in the world around them. We practice writing small on the very first day of class as I ask students to record the details of the room, the sounds, the odd shapes, the smells. I ask them to count things, the tiles on the floor, the number of people wearing sneakers, the number of people who are left-handed or are wearing glasses. I ask them to notice how their classmates write, hold their pen, or compose. To pick up these details, students must spy on one another, sneak sidelong glances in furtive ways so that others don't notice, and then record the details.

I sometimes read my own entries, particularly on the first days of class when students might be reticent about reading their work aloud. Here is an example of my own spying on my students.

9/15 It's a chilly Friday afternoon, the weather almost mid-October and white puffy clouds slowly drift under brilliant blue as 29 students and their teacher bend to their writing. No more than three feet away from me, but separated by a cinderblock wall, Mr. Newcombe dramatizes a scene from the mythology book for his ninth grade class.

On the window side of the wall, Claire is turned toward the window, her notebook open in front of her as she etches words onto the paper, holding her pen very low to the point. The writing she produces is small and crisp and neat, like the inscription on top of the head of a pin. Her Avion water bottle sits in front of her notebook, almost hiding her as she slouches low to look at the sky.

Many students in rows turn their heads to the right to peek at the other side of the room, though a few only swivel their eyes that way. They all hope to catch their classmates in interesting acts of posing.

It is in the writer's notebook that students record all sorts of details in the next ten months, piling things up in one and even two notebooks the way one might throw clippings and scraps into a compost heap. We talk about how these rich, organic scraps might have little value at the moment but may, in time, be converted into good soil for growing rich, fertile pieces of writing, often poems.

Expectations

I have told students that twenty pages of writing in their writer's notebook each quarter is a reasonable expectation. As they record the wide-awake moments in their lives, some of these pages will be accomplished in class while others will be done by them on their own time. We do quick writes from time to time and we write experiments that result from some of my minilessons. Periodically, they will go back to their writer's notebook and reread the pages, seeing if any topics emerge for them to develop into finished pieces.

I show them one poem that I wrote and trace its origin in my writer's notebook. I start by showing them a photocopy of a quick scribbling that I wrote one July day after a phone call from my daughter, Stacy. Then I tell them how I wrote a poem a few days later about Stacy's pregnancy and gave her the poem as a little present about four weeks later when she came for a visit. When I showed her a copy of the first version of the poem, she seemed pleased at my effort but wasn't jumping for joy. When she returned home the next day, the poem remained on the coffee table in the living room. I had a feeling that the pregnancy was a little too new for her and she wasn't quite ready to celebrate. In the meantime, I went back to the poem and began to revise a bit. When we visited Stacy and Chuck in Yardley, Pennsylvania, in late September, she was by then three months pregnant. Stacy and my wife, Eileen, were huddled outside at the picnic table on the patio, talking about baby furniture, clothing, and the like, when suddenly, she turned to me and asked if I still had that poem I had written earlier. Eileen

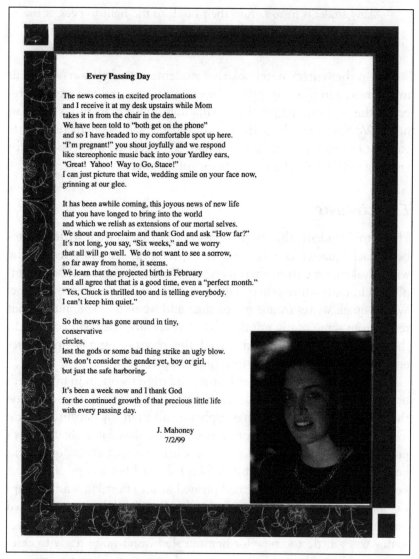

Every Passing Day

The news comes in excited proclamations
and I receive it at my desk upstairs while Mom
takes it in from the chair in the den.
We have been told to "both get on the phone"
and so I have headed to my comfortable spot up here.
"I'm pregnant!" you shout joyfully and we respond
like stereophonic music back into your Yardley ears,
"Great! Yahoo! Way to Go, Stace!"
I can just picture that wide, wedding smile on your face now,
grinning at our glee.

It has been awhile coming, this joyous news of new life
that you have longed to bring into the world
and which we relish as extensions of our mortal selves.
We shout and proclaim and thank God and ask "How far?"
It's not long, you say, "Six weeks," and we worry
that all will go well. We do not want to see a sorrow,
so far away from home, it seems.
We learn that the projected birth is February
and all agree that that is a good time, even a "perfect month."
"Yes, Chuck is thrilled too and is telling everybody.
I can't keep him quiet."

So the news has gone around in tiny,
conservative
circles,
lest the gods or some bad thing strike an ugly blow.
We don't consider the gender yet, boy or girl,
but just the safe harboring.

It's been a week now and I thank God
for the continued growth of that precious little life
with every passing day.

                    J. Mahoney
                    7/2/99

Figure 3–1 "Every Passing Day"

quickly said that she had saved the copy, but I said that the poem had changed since then and that I would get the revised copy to her.

As October and November passed, I began planning on turning this poem into a special gift, something my students and I had done numerous times before. In early December, my wife held a surprise baby shower, which seemed the perfect time to give my gift (see Figure 3–1). I put the poem printed on special paper and with just the right photo inside the picture frame, wrapped it, and tucked it in the mounting pile of presents. Stacy was so touched that she asked me to read it aloud. When she returned home, she placed the picture on a wall in her bedroom.

This gift celebrated the news of the first child, not diminishing the arrival of the next two children she had. The moment of finding out our daughter was pregnant is fixed in time, but the gift only came about because I took time to record it in my writer's notebook, taking a few minutes to "write small." But, not everything that goes into the writer's notebook ends up getting published in a finished piece, at least not at the time. Some of it, though, might easily be showcased somewhere.

Reflecting and Writing

Many of the pieces in my writer's notebook have come from my writing while students are writing in their notebooks or before class when I am preparing by trying first what they will write. However, these pieces are somewhat contrived because I am a teacher thinking about either motivating my students or providing a model. I sometimes ask myself, Do I, would I, write if it weren't for these teacherly things? But I discover in paging through my writer's notebook that I have entries of things that struck me at the time and I just felt like recording them, getting the details down before they fade away. I wrote the following one December day when I was grading portfolios for my community college class.

> It comes in all different ways—and when you least expect it. Just when your body aches and you want to lie down and take a nap rather than grade college portfolios, you take two aspirins instead, sit down, pull out a portfolio blindly, and open.
>
> There it is—the "Special Thanks" from the girl, Sue, who has worked through many issues, including her eating disorder that went back to her childhood and her swimming coach ridiculing her each time she stepped on the scale and showed a weight gain. She thanks me for teaching her much about writing and much about herself. It was her favorite class, she says and she says that I have a "bubbly" personality. Hmmm, maybe I do!

So now I must gather up the strength and pursue this pile of portfolios to find the hidden person and writer in each one.

And, too, there's Mande who wrote about her father's death in such poignant detail that her mother and aunt cried.

I was fortunate to be able to preserve those thoughts as a reminder of the thrill of seeing what students have been able to articulate in their lives. I find that having a pen and at least some kind of paper handy is a great key to writing small and recording the wide-awake moments on a life. But sometimes I don't have pen or paper handy as was the case one March afternoon when I was doing work in the backyard while listening to a tape of Robert Scholes at the previous NCTE convention. Something popped into my mind that I wanted to record so I rushed into the house and found a piece of note paper and a pen and I wrote the following words.

Sometimes it's just a little line that hops into your head at the oddest times, like when you're out back, cutting out the ivy that's growing up the neighbor's fence, and with a wire cutter, you're snipping off whole sections of a second fence of chicken wire to get a clear shot of the ivy, and Robert Scholes is talking on a tape from the convention about two poems of loss—and there it is—the line that pops into your head—but you don't have any way to write it down so it slowly fades and lingers on the fringes of your consciousness, along with the loss you were thinking of and now can't remember.

I keep hundreds of these little snippets in my writer's notebook because I have frequently forgotten an intention to turn them into little poems the way William Stafford did. He wrote early in the morning, every day, saying that he liked to write "little poems" in a regular sort of way. Every once in a while, I take one of these snippets and show my students how I craft it into a poem. It doesn't take very long, seven or eight minutes, once I have the original writing entry on a transparency. I show them how I start by breaking the prose into lines of a poem and deleting, changing, and more often adding words and phrases as I go. Sometimes I find that I need a final line to bring unity or closure to the work and then I write a title, often asking students for suggestions.

I then ask them to page through their writer's notebooks and find a short entry that they can craft into a poem in the next few minutes. When I ask for any volunteers to share something they've done, I usually find a person or two. We applaud and move on. What is important here is that I've modeled for them how to turn an entry into a poem, followed by them doing so. We've listened and learned, and then moved on. Perhaps in a conference later in the period, other students will show me what they wrote or maybe I won't see it until it is turned in as part of their quarterly portfolio. (For an explanation of quarterly portfolios, see *Power and Portfolios*).

After a particularly harsh winter, Sheila, a ninth grader in Jerry's class, went out into her backyard one afternoon and felt the sun's warmth on the back of her neck. After this realization, she began to notice everything, loving whatever her eyes could take in, much the way Whitman did. She saw the light, clear sky, the waves as they lapped against the shore below her raised yard, everything that called out to her. She heard the sound of "bird gossip" as she walked around, feeling "crispy yet soft grass" under her bare feet. As she lay sprawled on her back, looking up at the sky, she started thinking of about colors and noticed that "they were everywhere—green grass, light blue sky, dark blue water, creamy sand, a fiery whitish-yellowish-orangish sun." It then occurred to her to record this in her writer's notebook. The following is the rest of the reflection that she wrote in her portfolio at the end of the year.

Anyway—so I was thinking about all of this stuff, when I started relating to myself. I thought how the sea looked like the color of my eyes (my dad told me that a few times), and I was basically observing colors, when words started coming to me—sentences like those of poems began to materialize in my head. This happens sometimes—I'll just be looking at something and these words will start coming to me—forming lines—forming short poems about some things that I look at. It's pretty cool. So these lines started coming to me and a poem began to form in my mind. After receiving a few stanzas, I ran into the house to get my writer's notebook, so that I could capture them all while they were still fresh in my mind. I couldn't let a single word slip away from me—words are so precious. I grabbed it and ran back outside as fast as I could, trying my best to avoid talking to anyone and going over the line in my head in my desperate effort to remember everything. Fortunately, I didn't lose any of it even though Mom insisted on telling me something "very important" before I went back out. So anyway, I sat down and started writing out the lines. I knew I had to do it out here so I would be surrounded by the mood and the view I needed. After putting down what I had already, I had to slow down and think and wait for the rest of the poem to come.

This is the poem that Sheila wrote as a result of her observing and recording.

Creation
When God made my eyes,
He dipped his great hands
Into the deepest ocean,
Lifted them,
Glistening,
And dripping with blue.
When God made my hair,
He walked through fields, kind with wheat,
And picked the strand most golden.
When God made my skin,
He stood before the most glorious sunset,
Waited
Until the sky glowed
The softest peach,
And swept his fingers gently
Through sun-warmed hues.
On a day kissed with Spring,
God gave me life—
He drank of the lightest,
Sweetest wind,
And bestowed into me
Breath.

        —Sheila Erimez

In her portfolio's reflection on "Creation," Sheila wrote:

What color would my hair be? And my skin? How should I end it? Strangely enough, everything came to me—all my questions were answered almost immediately—as if by some supernatural force. I love it when you are trying to write a good poem and it comes out really wonderful. This is my favorite and well-written poem this year.

That part about "fields kind with wheat" came from *The Odyssey*—the line was originally "fields kind with grain." And the part about God drinking the wind actually came from a book I read on horses. There is a type of horse called an Arabian—one of the most beautiful and admired. The book said that long ago, the Indians used to call their Arabians "drinkers of the wind" because of the way they carried their heads. All of these things came together with my own thoughts and that other force that supplied my words. I wonder how that happened? I think God has given me a great ability—the ability to be inspired by nature. I believe we are all elements of nature—there are many different parts of it in all of us.

A Writing State of Mind

Sheila was able to do what I had failed to do in my backyard: capture words and phrases. We both went and got paper and pen to record our thoughts but Sheila took more time to bring back the words. I chose to record the details of my surroundings, mention my lost thoughts about loss, and get back to work. Sheila worked to restore the mood and view. I might have replayed the Scholes tape but I didn't. Sheila and I were both in a "writing state of mind," knowing enough to try and record what we thought were good ideas. The difference is that Sheila has a poem and I don't.

These examples are typical of what happens when students keep a writer's notebook. They become aware of needing to record observations and to write about events even when they are doing other things. Jeanine, an eleventh grader in my class, saw her writer's notebook as a means of taking a break from her homework and calming her nerves by writing about the sudden rain storm. From her entry, she later crafted the following poem that she included in her final portfolio.

> **Breathing Wind**
> Perched on the overstuffed couch,
> soft illumination hits the page
> on my musty text book.

Rain pounds against my skylight
in a fit of rage.
I listen,
in awe of the magnificent power of the heavens.
Barley audible,
I hear the sound of
precipitation streaming down the gutters,
creating crisp collisions
with muddy water
standing on the ground.
Wind that whips through trees
tunnels down the chimney,
forcing open the fireplace door.
Ashes spew out, covering the hardwood floor.
Dusty remnants whirl through the air
As I leap to shut the door.

Soon the pounding rain dies down
to reveal the soft sound of guitar
and wind
now distantly breaking through the trees.

—*Jeanine Beatty*

In her reflection about how this poem came about, Jeanine revealed that she had her writer's notebook nearby and was able to record what she was feeling and observing.

Late one February night, I sat staring blankly at the immense amount of homework that I had to complete by the following day. All of a sudden, the silent house was overcome by the sound of rain pounding against the skylight. I looked up from my textbook and witnessed this "magnificent power of the heavens." Carefully observing every action of the rain and wind, especially the force of the wind down the chimney, I took out my writer's notebook and recorded as much as I could. From these observations evolved my poem, "Breathing Wind."

When everything died down, I turned back to my homework, rejuvenated. Ignoring the foul smell of my textbook, I continued, feeling completely comfortable in my task; no more shifting in my seat, rubbing my dry eyes or trying to force myself to concentrate.

I am proud of this poem for many reasons, the first being the images it created for the reader, especially those of the water "creating crisp collisions." I also like it because it took an often used topic and gave it a new twist by focusing on the wind instead of the ordinary rain.

Without a writer's notebook, my students would not have a place that they can turn to, where they can record on the spot their precise observations and then store those details for safekeeping to be used at a later date. A writer's notebook reinforces memory.

4

Quick Writes and Observing

A Predictable Classroom Structure

Some years ago at an NCTE conference, I heard Tom Romano explain quick writes, something he learned from Linda Rief. I brought this writing activity to my own students after trying it at Tom's session and have used it ever since. I start every class with three prompts, partially written on the board, and as the bell rings to start class, I announce, "Take out your writer's notebooks and let's get started. Put today's date at the top of the page and here is the first quick write: 1. *I still remember the soft sound of his/her voice.* If you want to change that to *harsh* or *cruel* or *friendly*, do so, but write to that prompt now. Write as rapidly as you can for one minute, trying to fill in as much concrete information as you can. Ready? Go!"

Students write intensely since they've been starting each class this way for several weeks. They are used to my voice after about thirty seconds, yelling like a coach whose players are running sprints, "Come on, thirty seconds left. Race that pen! It's on fire! Make it fly across the page!" With fifteen seconds left, I'll do the same, urging them to "dig it out, dig it out" for the last few words. Then I'll call out, "Stop! Skip a line and write number 2." I'll go back to the board and point out prompt number 2, partially written as I complete it: *The sun was so hot that day that. . . .* I ask them to copy the prompt, but tell them to feel free to make a change, even suggesting something like *The sun shone so brilliantly that day . . .* or, *was so fierce that day. . . .* I remind them that we are not trying to write anything necessarily good or poetic, just trying to get stuff poured out into the writer's notebook for later use. Quantity of images and information is key, not how nice it sounds. I also remind them that the average adult, as well as student, can produce about five

26

lines of text in one minute, and I challenge them to produce more than that. "Ready, Go!" Again, I cheer them on at the thirty-second mark and then with ten or fifteen seconds left; I ask them to stop when the minute is up, telling them to skip a line and start writing prompt number 3 on the next line.

As I go to the board for the third quick write, I remind them of the great job they are doing in getting their brain so active right at the start of class, that they are actually improving their brain function every time they write so intensely. I read the third prompt, *I was very frightened that day*, and again offer them the opportunity to change this any way they want. As they are writing, I remind them that they are free to go off on a different tangent right in the middle of their quick write if something pops into their head. I tell them that they can always come back to the images they produced in the first thirty seconds but the second thirty may produce a topic that is infinitely more important to them. "Ready, Go!" And the process continues for the third and final time in the period.

This exercise works for any way a class is organized, but for me these four or five minutes at the start of every period are a great way of getting right down to work with no nonsense or wasting time. Students value it because it is quick and it allows them to fill up pages in their writer's notebook, bringing them closer to the expected twenty pages. They write about a page a day and I continue this exercise for several weeks. After the first month of school, I begin to back off with the daily quick writes, perhaps doing them two or three times a week. I ask students to write on their own time so that they don't become dependent on this opening activity as the only way they write in their notebooks. My first reason for doing quick writes is to increase fluency. At the start of the school year, there are some students who cannot sustain writing for one minute, and, judging by the number of heads that pop up before the minute, I may call stop and move on to the next one. I don't want students looking around or being a distraction. I want the weaker writers to feel that they are in the game, as much as the other stronger writers. In time, I will actually stretch the one minute longer, sometimes to two and three minutes. I can do this because my students have been working out their writing muscles regularly, building up their writing stamina. Visitors who have come to our classes are amazed at the ability of our students to write intensely for sustained periods of time.

The primary function of this writing activity is to generate material, *stuff* we call it, that might be used for a variety of writing purposes during the quarter and the year. I remind my students that all writers keep writer's notebooks to build up material for use in writings not yet conceived. So the students are doing what real writers, including poets, do. These materials are, as I've said earlier, like matter that is added to a compost heap of things written on separate occasions, that place where organic matter is mixed with other organic matter and allowed to sit for a while.

New Quick Writes

For a long time, I used the three prompts for quick writes to start each class. However, Linda Rief (2003) suggested another way to begin the period with quick writing, one not so intense or frenetic as the three one-minute prompts. Linda showed us how to take a single poem, distribute it to the class, read it to them, and then ask them to pick out their own lines as prompts for their writing.

As an example, I recently photocopied two poems, "What I Learned from My Mother," by Julia Kasdorf and "To be of use," by Marge Piercy, for this activity. The first poem begins with the poet telling how her mother had extra vases on hand in case she had to visit a friend in the hospital and wanted to take flowers. Marge Piercy's poem tells how the speaker loves most people who take on work with gusto, not waiting around for orders. Between these two poems, students have more than enough to choose from. They take more time getting started because they often read over the poem, or sections of it, before writing. I tell them that they have two minutes for each quick write rather than the one minute and I don't call out times. Before beginning, I instruct them to stop at the end of the two minutes and find a new prompt, even though they will want to continue their present writing. With discipline, they learn to break away to find a new prompt and are glad that they did so because they have that many more ideas in their writer's notebook.

Scaffolding as a Help

One advantage of this self-selecting approach is that it brings students back into texts and allows them to examine the lines before finding their own way. There are some students who are not as skilled or as comfortable in finding their own lines. I write on the board some of the lines that might be good prompts and allow students to use these just as they did with the one-minute quick writes. Some, whether students with special needs or just convinced nonwriters, have a hard time with the one-minute versions and don't know how to develop an unfinished prompt. They get very frustrated trying to write rapidly in such a short period of time. For these students, I supply three prompts from the poem on an index card, asking the writer to pick any one line or more that they would like. This eases the pressure and usually allows him or her to write something useful.

Creating Independence Through Observation

If I restricted the use of the writer's notebook to only quick writes and prompts, students would continue to be dependent on me for their writing and topics. Earlier, I explained how on the first day of class students recorded their observations of the world around them. After a day or two, I introduce a new concept, such as the thoughts going on in their minds as they write about their observations. I tell them that most poets deal with the outer and inner self, the things going on around them as well as the thoughts and feelings occurring inside them. I show them a short poem by Li-Young Lee (2001) called "Praise Them," and we identify the outer and inner elements. Lee begins in the first two lines by identifying the birds and shows how they don't change space but simply reveal it. Later, he indicates that the birds are the nervous ones and wonders about the possibility of even one usually violent person being gentle. We conclude that there is the observable—the birds—but there are the thoughts about the birds and their connection to the poet. The class returns to their observations, but this time to record what is going on inside their heads as well as what they are observing around them. Here they might include their nervousness on the first day of school or the first day of this class, or their excitement at the writing activity.

Writing Provinces

In the back of their writer's notebook, students keep several blank pages labeled Writing Provinces. We define a province as an area or a

29

territory, an undefined space. In this section, students keep an ongoing list of topics they could write about in the future. When we finish setting up this list, I move students into groups of three to discuss their observations of the quick writes. They need not read what they have written, though most read something, but they do need to explain their topics and how they came to choose them. I tell the students that they are to listen to others for possible topics they could use and, when they hear one, turn to their Writing Provinces section and record the topic. This is one way to show them they are able to find topics to write about on their own, independent of me. In time, they come to see that they can get topics from poems they read, from the world, and from listening to the writing of their classmates. In this way, I hope to create independent writers who do not have to rely on their teachers for ideas about writing.

During the first week of class, I take a lot of time to establish the writer's notebook. In this process, students have read from poems, used lines of poetry to inspire their own writing, practiced observing and recording, set up their writing provinces, listened to each other talk about their writing, and obtained additional topics to write about. They were highly engaged during all of this time.

Remembrance of Things Past
Early Memories

Jerry Matovcik

Memory is a wellspring of ideas for poems, a deep source that rises up with the least provocation. One recalls the moment the narrator of Marcel Proust's *Remembrance of Things Past* tastes a morsel of a petite madeleine cake after it was dipped in a cup of tea—a treat his Aunt Leonie gave him as a child—and the taste causes his childhood home, the town of Combray, the square, the streets, and the country roads he ran on as a boy suddenly to spring to mind. Guided writing is the sip of tea from which memories spring.

After some guided writing, Rachel, an eleventh grader, recalls the memory of the lake house she visited as a young girl, unfolding layers of lost time to reconnect with an earlier time of innocence.

The Lake House
Antsy in the backseat of a rusted maroon Volvo
On the long ride to the lake house,
We were so much younger then . . .

Racing you to the front door,
I bounded inside, a victorious marathon runner.
We shot rock-paper-scissors for the top bunk bed
With cozy flannel sheets and the Rainbow Brite bedspread.
Exploring expeditions all day:
On paddle boats and wooden rafts,
Discovering turtle habitats and bird nests,
Basking in the stillness of harmonic nature,
Whistling a glorious tune.

We escaped nightly to the loft
With its vaulted ceilings and vast skylights,
A glimpse of the midnight galaxy above us.
We hardly slept at all,
Choosing instead to spend our nights
Professing undying love to junior-high boys
But only in secret notes we hid in the old ceiling beams.

Stewart's was unforgettable—
    Roller skates,
    Homemade root beer,
    Foot-long hot dogs with "the works"

But my favorite moments were the ones quietly passed
At the hearth of the fireplace,
The flames warming our hands,
Friendship warming our hearts,
As we pondered the way only children do,
A future as carefree as our delightful past.
We were so much younger then . . .

Now, I'm terrified of heights (especially top bunk beds).
My Rainbow Brite memorabilia has been discarded with disdain.
I wouldn't dream of clogging my arteries with a foot-long pork product.
Sixteen years often seems too old.

Now, I drown, attached to anchors of priorities and expectations.
I wish to reach up into those old ceiling beams and
Delicately unfold tattered looseleaf and layers of lost time
To reconnect with
Two little girls,
Best friends,
A marvelous childhood, and
The lake house.

—*Rachel Santoro*

Generally, when Jim and I have our students write about happy memories, we notice that they often go back to times of innocence, times when they were young and free of the cares and worries that they have come to experience as young people in high school. They relish those earlier days and find it both joyful and elusive at they try to pin down the colors and sounds and feelings of their romping and cavorting. Meghan, a ninth grader, recalled such days in her poem, "The Thrill of the Chase."

The Thrill of the Chase
The summer sun beats down
On the freshly cut sod,
Diffusing joy to our souls.
Blades of grass slip through my toes.
I leap across the fields barefoot,
Chasing my younger sister
In a game of tag.
The late morning sun hovers overhead
As a brisk breeze blows by,
Carrying with it a scent of honeysuckle and lilac.
I chase her from behind,
Both of us in gay, matching sundresses—
White and pink, patterned delicately with hearts.
I grasp her dress with my fingertips,
Yelling, "You're it!"
Out of breath,
I turn and run toward the golden sun.
I feel her heavy breath on my neck as she approaches.
We are happy together—
An unusual feeling for us now.

But as I look back on that one summer day,
We were bonded together
By the sun shining above and
The thrill of the chase.

—*Meghan Delaney*

Angel, as a ninth grader, wrote a short poem about her aunt's cooking and how her spaghetti sauce remains fixed in her memory.

Aunt Millie's Homestyle
A heart overflows with love
Like a pot
of spaghetti sauce
on the kitchen floor.

You try and wipe it up
but that stain never goes away.
—Angel Lloyd

Getting Started

As I write on the board, "Exploring Happy Memories—Recalling Times of Innocence and Joy," I ask students to open their writer's notebooks to record the memories that they will recollect. I ask them to list several times in their earliest years when they can remember being very happy. Then I ask them to close their eyes, even lower their heads on their arms on the desktops, and relax their bodies, allowing all of the tension of the day to subside. I ask them to think of one of the happy moments from their list, and I begin to ask the following questions that appeal to one of the five senses about these recollections.

Sight. Where are you? Who is present? What are they wearing? How are you dressed? Are you inside or outside? What do you see around you? What colors come to mind? What are you doing, just sitting or doing some activity? What time of day is it and what month of the year?

Touch. What is the texture of things? Can you feel the cushion or the sand you sit on? Can you feel the bark of the tree you lean against or the mud you play in? What is the weather like? Do you feel the heat or the wind or the breeze or the cold snow?

Smell. Do you smell anything, like perfume, aftershave lotion, a pipe, something cooking, the ocean smell, dry leaves, or newly cut grass?

Sound. What sounds do you hear? Is anyone talking, arguing, singing, laughing? Is there a radio or TV on in the background? Can you hear birds singing, crickets chirping, or the ocean pound on the sand? Can you hear street traffic, a subway or bus, or planes taking off?

Taste. Do you taste anything like ice cream, spaghetti sauce, hot tea?

After taking students through this process for ten to twelve minutes, I ask them to open their eyes slowly as they adjust to the lights. Then, turning to their writer's notebook, they jot down as many details as they can, not worrying about telling the story coherently but instead recording the sense impressions that they have pulled from their memory. They write for about ten minutes and then form groups of three in which they share their early memory. I write on the board under the word "Feedback":

1. *Strong Images.* Tell what you could easily picture from the retelling.
2. *More Information.* Tell where you would like more detail.

I explain that the first job of the two students in the group who are listening is to tell the writer what images or details they can best understand or feel. Their second task is to point out places that need more information, places where they want the writer to give more information.

After about fifteen minutes, I ask for volunteers to share some strong details they heard as they listened in their groups. I want writers to hear their peers recall powerful images. Volunteers report on incidents that they could relate to because they had a similar experience as the writer. Students return to their writer's notebooks and list any early memories of their own that were sparked from the stories that others told. I remind them that their writing topics during the year will mostly come from their own choices and that they should build up a stockpile of these topics by listening to the writing of their classmates.

At this point, the class period is usually over. The next day, my minilesson is on revision, using several drafts of a poem, showing how the writer cuts out words and phrases, getting down to the essential images. I kid that for every unnecessary word we can eliminate, the writer gets a dollar. Students find it hard to do this paring down at first because they fall in love with all of their words. They also want to include every detail that they remember in their own experience for the readers's full understanding.

As a result of the probing we do at the beginning of the year, students realize those early memories contain rich material to mine for pieces of writing. After a while, they don't need the structure that we first used. The following poem by Mary, an eleventh grader, which was prompted by her reading of a poem by Seamus Heaney, is the result of the mining of an early memory. (See Chapter 6, Gift Poems.)

Child of the Field
What she remembers is the sound of the old whistle
As it trails off into the back of her mind.
In her head, she knows it is the end of the game.

In her heart, she yearns to hold on to the end,
As if it were the beginning.
She remembers the cluttered circle of six year olds
Kicking wildly at her feet.
The voices of the parents, echoing what their hearts long to say,
Echo in her ears.
The fresh October air cleansed their innocent souls
As they ran.
They will always play on in her mind,
whenever she remembers.

—Mary Zoccoli

Mary wrote a reflection about the source of her poem—the Pee Wee soccer league—and how the joy of soccer resided in the play on the field with her friends and in the sound of their parents laughing on the sidelines.

> "Child of the Field" came about when Mr. Mahoney introduced to us the idea of beginning a poem with "She or he remembers." I really thought that this could turn out to be an interesting piece so I began to think back into my childhood, searching for something that I would want to show the reader was meaningful to me. Instantly, I thought of my pee-wee soccer days so that is what I wrote about. Everyone's parents yelled in laughter from the sidelines, seeming so proud of us. I always felt so good after those games, win or lose. I remember it being so much fun to play with and against my friends. It is funny that to this day I am still playing with and against those same friends. It really was a great time that I will never forget.

In *Teaching with Fire: Poetry That Sustains the Courage to Teach,* a collection of essays, teachers explain how a poem has been important to their teaching or their personal lives (Dean 2003). Primary school teacher Sandra Dean selected the poem "First Reader" by Billy Collins, and in her explanation cites children's writer Edith Nesbit, who said that as a child she used to "pray fervently, tearfully, that when she should grow up, she might never forget what she thought, felt, and suffered as a child" (24). In other words, poetry conveys empathy for a child's thoughts and emotions, reminding teachers that concern for a child's well-being holds primacy over concern for the classroom lessons they teach. Dean adds, "These poems invite us to retrieve the fragile memories of childhood so that we can work with more heart and wisdom as adults" (24). Jim and I would say that poetry not only helps teachers to work with more heart and wisdom but it allows students to gain some of that heart and wisdom as well. Mary Zoccoli has seen that from her poetry.

6

Gift Poems

The scene is almost archetypal: a small boy takes the big steps down from the school bus, one at a time, one hand gripping the shiny pole, the other hand holding up some colored papers, excitement bubbling from his eyes. No sooner do his feet hit the ground than the child heads for his waiting mother, waving the papers, saying, "Mommy, look at the picture I made for you for Thanksgiving!" The mother hugs her little boy and examines the picture and the story, smiling, expressing great glee for each detail. She tells him that they will have to show this to others in the family and then they will hang it on the refrigerator or the bulletin board for all to admire. They head home to set up the exhibit of the child's work.

Change the one getting off the bus to a little girl, the one waiting for a father, grandparent, or sibling, the arrival from bus to opening the door of the house, or the day to any holiday or special occasion. What doesn't change is the joy of giving and the happiness at receiving, especially when the accomplished work is made public. It is not at all unusual for these precious gifts to be stored for many years—in a drawer, closet, trunk, or other place of safekeeping.

Fast-forward eight, ten, twelve, or more years and watch that same child come to the waiting parent, grandparent, sibling, friend, or beloved with a gift of writing, a poem or recollection, in a picture frame, tastefully wrapped as a present. Is the excitement of the giver or the receiver any less than it had been years ago? Is the admiration any less sincere? Would the desire to display the work in a place of prominence diminish over the years? Unfortunately, schools do not foster such work for students as they move up the grade levels; teachers forget about the joy of giving and receiving as they immerse their students in "the curriculum"; students don't have opportunities to use their advanced talents to give gifts of their work, and parents, grandparents, and other potential recipients never get the chance to receive such gifts.

They don't, unless teachers show students and value it enough to make it part of their "curriculum." Our term for this is *writing as gifts* and our students write with the option of giving the piece as a gift. Forty to 50 percent of our students give writing as gifts in some way, even if it's just reading it to another person. Others carry the practice all the way to fancy paper, adding a picture or image to enhance the writing, and containing the work in a frame. And it all began with a tribute to a dog.

The Dog Story

A story I've told in *Power and Portfolios* seems worth repeating here. I'm not particularly fond of dogs, but my wife knew that kids growing up with dogs was a good thing and overrode any mild protests I might make. One special dog was Coco, a mix of German Shepherd and Lab, who became the primary responsibility of our son Tim when he was nine years old. Coco followed Tim everywhere, including places where the two played soccer. This puppy grew up around a soccer ball and eventually learned to chest trap balls in the air, to stop shots Tim would make at an imaginary net, and to dribble the ball back to Tim so he could drive the ball and send Coco racing after it once again. Coco adapted to other sports, fielding tennis balls used as pucks for street hockey games and racing after other kids in touch football games in front of the house, acting as a defensive halfback.

One of the saddest days of my life was the drizzly April evening, some twelve years later, when Tim and I carried Coco into the vet's office to have her euthanized. Earlier in the day, my older son, Brian, working in a Florida office, received the bad news about Coco from Tim. While we were at the vet with Coco, Brian was sitting at his desk in tears, writing a poem, which he would eventually send home, about Coco and his own sorrow, living so far away from home.

> **The Last One in for Supper**
> Informed at work
> By a "While You Were Out,"
> The distance seemed much further
> Than 'long distance.'
> "Your dog," it said, "Call home."

Recent Christmases,
Like Dickens' final Ghost,
Had promised this: the
Howard Hughes routine,
Beneath a blanket in the corner
Of the furthest room,
The leglessness, the sniping
At fleas that weren't there.

Today, another childhood
Is harder to keep track of,
Like wiffleballs of last at-bats,
Landing somewhere in the aging dusk,
While mothers and streetlights
Announce supper

She tended nets, she
Tripped up undisputed touchdowns, she
Fielded wiffleballs no one could see,
Padding down the block to save
The game before it rolled
Into the sewer.

She was the last one in for supper,
Always. While I was out, she padded
Off, down the block,
Out of distant streetlight's
Age old limit, into
The God-forsaken schoolnight.

She left a man three thousand miles
Away, pretending to work late,
Crying at his desk, for more at-bats,
Against the God-forsaken school night,
Unable to come home for supper.

—*Brian Mahoney*

Shortly after this event, Brian sent us a copy of the poem he had written about Coco's death. When my wife, Eileen, read it, she asked me to put it on fancy paper as we had done so often with student writing. I typed it on nice paper with an attractive border, thinking that was enough, but she seemed to want something more. In the meantime, I shared the poem with Jerry and he in turn showed it to all of his classes.

Six months later, as we were approaching Christmas, I passed the guidance office where Jerry was working with Chris, a ninth grader, to create a paper that had a poem about his dog that had died. The two of them were cutting out a circle where they were going to place a picture of Chris' father and the dog. They were planning on using designer paper, putting the paper in a picture frame, and having Chris give this to his father as a Christmas present.

With Chris' gift poem in mind, I decided to do the same thing with Brian's poem. I found three different pictures of Coco, my wife, and Tim, and I created, on Christmas Eve morning, three separate gifts, one for Eileen, one for Tim, and one for Brian. I bought three picture frames and prepared all three gifts. (See Figure 6–1.) The next morning, as my wife began to open some of her presents, she found my gift.

The Last One In For Supper

Informed at work
By a "While You Were Out,"
The distance seemed much further
Than "long distance."
"Your dog," it said, "Call home."

Recent Christmases
Like Dickens' final Ghost,
Had promised this; the
Howard Hughes routine,
Beneath a blanket in the corner
Of the furthest room,
The leglessness, the sniping
At the fleas that weren't there.

Today, another childhood
Is harder to keep track of,
Like wiffleballs of last at-bats,
Landing somewhere in the aging dusk,
While mothers and streetlights
Announce supper.

She tended nets, she
Tripped up undisputed touchdowns, she
Fielded wiffleballs no one could see,
Padding down the block to save
The game before it rolled
Into the sewer.

She was the last one in for supper,
Always. While I was out, she padded
Off, down the block,
Out of distant streetlight's
Age old limit, into
The God-forsaken schoolnight.

She left a man three thousand miles
Away, pretending to work late,
Crying at his desk, for more at-bats,
Against the God-forsaken school night,
Unable to come home for supper.

— Brian Mahoney

Figure 6–1 "The Last One in for Supper"

She read the poem silently, tears sliding down her cheeks. Then she said softly to me, "This is the best Christmas present of all."

When our vacation was over, I convinced my wife to let me take the gift to school for a short time, to show my students. They were moved by the gift poem and the story, and it wasn't long before I was seeing gift poems about cats, dogs, other pets, and even deceased grandparents and relatives.

Double Gifts

In September 2002, we moved 130 miles to the south, from Long Island to Yardley. It wasn't that far, really, just a two-and-a-half-hour drive up the New Jersey Turnpike, over the Verazanno Bridge, and out to St. James. In Yardley, I could even hear about New York sports on my favorite radio station, WFAN. I wasn't that far from home, and our daughter, Stacy, lived in the same town. But, boy, was I sad. I had left my roots, my friends, my parish church just a block away, Tim and Debbie and their two children, but most of all, I had this sense that my children and especially my son Brian had no real place from childhood to come home to.

At our new home that September day, I stood opening the mail in an empty kitchen, first a big box with two picture frames sent to us from Brian. Each frame, one for my wife and one for me, contained a different poem with an accompanying picture. I looked first at the frame for my wife and saw a color picture of the four bedroom colonial house we had just left and a poem under it entitled "My Parents' House." I read the first stanza quickly:

> My parents' house was my house too,
> The place where I became.
> They sold my house, my starting place,
> But only time's to blame.

I couldn't read any more, my eyes filling with tears, and I turned away, passing both frames to my wife, walking away to another empty room. Eventually, I came back but could not bring myself to read the two poems. I did read the short note that Brian had sent along, explaining the origin of both poems. The one for me contained "Well Coached" and a picture of my three children taken a few weeks before-hand when we had a farewell party for the house and neighborhood.

He explained that Eileen had asked him to write a poem to me for Father's Day because she noticed how sad I was feeling at the idea of moving. Brian said that he got tied up in his own school year closing and couldn't finish it in time for the June date, but he thought this would be a good present now. Since I had coached all three children in different sports when they were younger, he wanted me to know that the "coaching lessons" had been well received and had become life lessons. He said that Tim and Stacy had each given him material about times when I had coached them so each had a stanza for a story. Once again, I could not bear to read the poem, because I got choked up.

Instead, I put both poems aside until the next afternoon when I decided to pack them in my bag and take them to the remedial writing class I had begun teaching a week earlier at DeVry University in Fort Washington. I wanted to introduce the idea of writing as gifts to my students so I took out both of Brian's poems and read them, for the first time, in front of my students. I was more composed this time and was able to read them through and to give the class a sense of how important these poems were to me. After that, I was able to structure a writing activity so they could also write their own gift poems. The two poems follow.

My Parents' House

My parents' house was my house too,
The place where I became.
They sold my house, my starting place,
But only time's to blame.

That place still stands where once we loved,
Looking much the same.
I can't return there anymore;
No one knows my name.

I have a photo on my wall
That memories fully frame.
My parents' house is always home,
Despite what time may claim.

Well Coached

We don't want another season passed,
Oak leaves once a supple new born green,

43

Now a leathered quilt upon a late September lawn.
Before another Series then, we need to thank you
For the Game you gave us, pitch by pitch,
Underhand at first, then true as we could handle.

When I whiffed then sniffed one GAL affair,
You enrolled me gently to Gaynor before
Grassy evening could dismiss my skills.
"No, Man, she can hit, later boys conceded.
Move back, her old man taught her."

And when I, "The Fireballer" went wild and weepy
On the hill, you said, "Armpit," so funny and so right,
Backstop bangers morphed into guided missile strikes.

And when rabid grounders bounded through my wickets,
You said to keep my nose and Billy Williams in the dirt,
And I snared a lot o' hot ones after that.

We wanted you to know your fundamentals stand.
We, well coaches, have put our Summer Game
To more than baseball ever since.

Getting Started

I have accumulated so many examples of gift poems that I wonder if I
sometimes overwhelm students by starting with these wonderful examples from others. As a result, sometimes I start right in with an activity that students can complete first and then I show them examples of
how their writing might be turned into a gift poem. Jerry and I have
two favorite approaches. The first is to give out a copy of a poem by
Seamus Heaney called "Mother of the Groom." I read it a few times
and point out how a mother sits in church at the wedding of her son
and recalls with great tenderness how he has grown and "slipped" from
her soapy hands as she gave him a bath when he was a small boy. It is
a poem about rings and celebrations, holding on and letting go, about
looking back and looking ahead. The poem begins with the third person pronoun, *She*, and recalls a ring of boots around the tub. I ask students to think about someone, living or dead, whom they want to
honor or remember and to begin by referring to themselves with the

third person pronoun, and saying, "What he remembers" or "What she remembers." So they write about themselves remembering the special person they've selected. Imitating the first line of Heaney's poem becomes a scaffold for the kind of details we are encouraging, "small writing" that captures the person being recalled and universalizes the details for others to embrace.

Magic Words

The other approach is to use a list of words that Jerry and I got from our friend and fellow English teacher Bill Picchioni (see Figure 6–2). I have changed the title to "Magic Words" because the words have such an amazing effect of producing images, unplanned for and even startling. We used to give this list to students and show them how to write down a word or phrase that seemed to jump off the page, adding words to it for as long as possible until the need arose to look for an additional word or phrase. The result was writing that sometimes seemed wild with disjointed images. Students have such fun with this exercise that they are usually eager to share their writing by reading it to the class. After their first writing in their writer's notebook, I ask them to try again but this time, to think of someone they want to recall or to honor. Then I ask them to look through the list for words that can get them started in writing the details about the person they are celebrating. The following poem was written by a middle-aged student in one of my college evening classes. When given the writing task, Reynald immediately thought of his sister who had had died some years earlier, a sister who had come with him from Haiti when they were young. After we had a conference about the poem, he went to a website for art and found a picture of an angel that he associated with his sister. Because he could not give the poem to any living member of his family, he simply placed the picture and the poem in his portfolio as a tribute to his sister.

> **Sister**
> Brave soldier, now angel,
> You fought deception
> And
> Conquered Death's sting.

Magic Words

sweet	spontaneous	snow spring	darling		buds
angry	garden of	earth	spinning	pushing	yellow
blue	birth	again	now	ground	wind	knife	moment

sweet   spontaneous   snow spring   darling   buds

angry   garden of   earth   spinning   pushing   yellow

blue   birth   again   now   ground   wind   knife   moment

God   bright   the sound of   trees   groan   living   flame

tulips   deep dark gold   and love and lovers   naughty   dimpled

dappled   the wide wild embrace   furious   rosebuds   in triumph

damp   wet loam   curling   sprinkled   fingers   wrinkled

wolf and swan   stars   rhythm   juice   passion   homeless   fire

time and time again   listen to the   ashes of youth   nourish   twilight

angels   the dead   answer   blue star   wingbeats   nights   in flight

sand the sun   the kiss of emerald   ancient incense   deception   O Muse

blaze coolly   whiteflowing gossamer gown   return   in secret   drink

the gift of grass and meadows and wildflowers all   swift and sweet   horrid

the grit of city streets swirling   blackness   dreamily dream   gloom

softly   body curve   snake   scent   in darkness dwelt   ruined feathers

marble words   faith   on his bed   the time of hurt   now and forever

cold canyon   like a steady engine   in the wilderness   snarl of stones   blue white

yes   the good, the rich   the stinging tears   ripe   falling stars and eagles   magic

charms   cobalt flowers   chrome glint gleam of car metal   hard   drunk   slick

sleek   smooth   rough   coarse splinters   mother   nectar   thoughts   death's sting

in the fields of youth   delicious   rest   and you, my dear   a signal   spilling fire

we are standing facing each other   a room of silver   your voice   radiate

Figure 6–2 Magic Words

In triumph, you fly above
The ardent flame of eternal fire
That
Now Angel, you fear no more.

Sing, dance, fly, and rejoice.
Happy to be free.
Happy to be angel.

—*Reynald St. Fleur*

Writing Inspires Writing

Sometimes students write gift poems to their teacher and include them in their portfolios. I have been fortunate to have received some and, with a sense of humility, include one here.

I Appreciate
He sits at his desk
as the sweat forms on his brow.
The dedication,
the time he put in,
puts in,
trickles down his puckered forehead
as he writes.

I begin to notice each wrinkle
representing each team,
each heart he touched,
mine, of course, one of them.
The years as my coach,
my mentor,
my teacher,
take up only a tiny place
in his immense heart.

He cries out silently
as he feels unappreciated,
unwanted.

Perhaps he needs to step back
and see the man who holds the hearts
of countless reckless soccer players,
the notebooks of school children,
and my soul.

—Mary Zoccoli

In the same spirit, because I think a poem can say so much, I have
written poems in response to portfolios that my students have written.
Sometimes I write my comments and include an appropriate poem by
a "famous" poet and sometimes I write my own poems to accompany
my prose comments. I always took additional time responding to the
portfolios of my eleventh graders because I knew that most of them
would be asking me for a college letter of recommendation in the fall,
a time when I would be busier than ever. To head them off, I decided
to use my detailed portfolio response as my recommendation to convey
my feelings about their reading and writing abilities.

Generally, I would read the portfolio through, often for the second
or third time, and I would take notes about specific pieces of writing,
or of strong language, or interesting themes. With some general
imagery in mind and the writer's theme, cover, and title, I would record
my impressions with specific references. Jeanine Beatty's portfolio,
called *Eternal Sunrise*, emphasized that the sun is always shining some-
place in the world, that it is always sunrise or sunset somewhere. Her
portfolio cover was done in black contact paper and had images of the
rising or setting sun. With that in mind, I wrote the following.

Black and Gold
The Grand Show—finally!
In all its splendor
the golden ball rises slowly before me
and reveals the mists and the valleys
of your mind.
I've had glimmers
and glimpses
but this is the reality
and I hold Eternal Sunrise in my hands
as if in prayer

and the words are the meditation
of the new day.

With care I turn each page,
reminded of our finite sunrises,
and wishing to linger longer
with each one of these days.
Your portfolio renews me
after double sessions
of late August on dry soccer fields
and all I want to do is be quenched.
Each page and every piece
is a fresh look
at the infinite possibilities
of a fertile mind,
and closing it each time, I am restored.

When strong feelings are put into writing and given with care to
another person, these words stand for more than just the emotions.
They show an effort to create a lasting tribute that will endure and
repeat those feelings for years to come.

7

Peer Conferencing and Revision
Revising Is Re-Seeing

Sometimes when I go to my workbench in the basement for a tool or a screw or a nail, I need to bring two pairs of glasses—my computer glasses for distance seeing and my reading glasses for close examination. Sometimes I may hardly need a light on at all because I know exactly where what I want is and could find it in the pitch dark. At other times, the basement light may not bright enough, and I will have to flick on the fluorescent light over the bench to see more clearly. Being able to see what you want, then, can be a tricky thing.

In writing, the ability to see and find just the right image or phrase may be as elusive as finding the right tool or screw. Writers can benefit from other eyes or more light. They can also learn by looking at the work done by their peers and learning how to make suggestions to the writers.

Revision Possibilities

To teach revision as seeing something again or anew instead of as correcting, I introduce peer revision as part of a process of writing a poem. I ask students to have a draft of a poem they've been working on completed by a specific day. I give them a handout called "Revising Is Re-Seeing—Four Things We Can Give to the Poet," which usually contains a clear poem written by a student from another class or another year. We talk about the need to be able to tighten up writing, expand, recast lines or phrases to change the emphasis, and add needed information or provide figurative language to make the writing clearer. On this handout, I have numbered each line of the poem, including the title. Underneath, I have listed, from A to D, four kinds of change that the writer could make—(A) changing words, (B) recasting, (C) adding a line or phrase, and (D) adding figurative language—along with the lines from the poem where the change could be made and the suggested revision. If the poet had written, "A cold brisk wind would blow," I might have written "l. 4, A cold wind would whip," emphasizing the change from *blow* to *whip* to help the alliteration of the words *wind would*. Below that example, I might also write, "l. 4, "a biting wind" to replace *cold brisk*, combining the two feelings of temperature and wind movement with the perhaps better image of a biting wind. These would be examples of the first type of revision, changing words.

In the second example, I might look at recasting a sentence to change the emphasis. The student may have written something like "A bucket of snowballs sits/ by the front door,/ waiting for an incoming attack." I would have written, "ll. 11–13, We set a bucket of snowballs by the front door, ready for an incoming attack." This suggestion changes the emphasis from the snowballs to the kids who took the time to make some snowballs ahead of time and left them in bucket by the front door.

Sometimes I can add a whole new line to further the image. The student may have written, "Body angels lay fresh in the clean snow," and I might add, "l. 16, "holding our fresh impressions," giving the idea that the kids themselves created the snow angels as another form of winter fun. This addition in the form of a participial phrase makes clearer what a body angel is and how it connects to the kids lying on their backs in the snow and waving their outstretched arms up and down to create the image of angel wings.

The last option is to add figurative language, most often through the use of a simile or a metaphor. If the student had concluded his poem by saying something like "I guess the snow has left me forever," I might write, "l. 19, I guess the snow, like birds from my childhood, has flown from my life forever." This shows how to add a simile and then to extend that flying image as it applies to the absence of the snow days of one's youth.

Pass the Paper

After spending about ten minutes reviewing this handout, I ask students to take out their poems, making sure their names are on the top, and number the lines. Then each person passes their poem to the person behind them and the person in the last seat brings his poem to the one in the front seat. I tell them they have about seven or eight minutes to suggest one of the four kinds of revisions we've just gone over. When they're done, I call for them to pass the poem again until we have done four or five peer suggestions for each poem. Then they return the poems to the original poet. I emphasize that they are free to take any, all, or none of the suggestions offered. As the writers, they are free to do that. However, they now have options given to them by other writers who have "seen" their poems with a different pair of glasses under different lighting conditions.

This activity gives students practice in re-seeing the work of others, helping them think about how it might be better. They read the suggestions that others have made, and they learn other ways to make suggestions. In the final minutes before the bell rings, students can also speak with others in the class about their work and they can have a conference about a suggested revision. These minutes spent have a great carryover as students return to their own poems and think about seeing things in a way that perhaps they hadn't seen before.

8

Writing an Extended Metaphor

While students enjoy writing about themselves and benefit from clarifying their lives and celebrating people and issues, they seem to dream of writing "really deep" poems. Most of them have been taught that great poems have deep meanings, expressed through symbols, yet they are often confused as to how their teachers are able to pull out those meanings, almost like rabbits from a hat. As a result, students want to have symbols and images in their poems. Writing an extended metaphor helps them create an image and sustain or extend it. Later, they can use that skill to write a poem in the form of an extended metaphor about someone they want to honor or write an extended metaphor about themselves in their portfolio.

I always begin with Carl Sandburg's famous poem "Fog" when I introduce the writing of an extended metaphor. Whether I am using "Fog" in a workshop with teachers or in a classroom with my students, I first ask what the fog is compared with, and we agree that this is both personification in the strictest sense and metaphor in the larger sense. We define simile at this time and agree that the comparison of the fog with a cat is direct and clear because the fog moves on "cat feet." The easy part is over. I then ask them to circle any other direct cat images and underline any indirect cat images or references and then to count them.

The fact is that there are no more direct cat images in the form of figurative language because there is nothing else in the poem that is limited just to a cat. We then look at other images of cats that we have in our head and ask why. *Sits* is the first word that comes up because we all can picture a cat sitting after walking, the way it tucks its legs under it and sits in such an upright position. But I ask what would happen if I changed the word *cat* in the second line to *dog* or *elephant*. Would the image of a cat sitting still remain in line three? We conclude that the picture of a cat in line two must still be in our heads when we get to line three and that that image helps to "extend" the first metaphor. The big problem for many is the word *haunches*. They swear that that is a direct reference to a cat until someone says that many animals have haunches, including the cat's prey, the mouse. So *haunches* becomes an indirect reference as does the expression *moves on*. We agree that you don't need the repetition of the initial image to have an extended metaphor. Then I show them one that I wrote.

A few years ago, my longtime friend Bill Picchioni asked us in a workshop on writing to write an extended metaphor and saying to someone, "You are a. . . ." I wrote a poem about my oldest son, Brian, who to me was "a game of catch" himself.

I had attempted to compare the ever-changing relationship of a father and his son to a game of catch, something Brian and I did from the time he was very young. Others in that writing session thought that I had captured the tension between a father and a son by the changes in the son's growth and how the father changed as well. I liked it as well, feeling I had expressed my love for my son by comparing it with the intimate "conversation" of a game of catch. I extended the impact of the poem by finding a current color picture of Brian with a baseball hat on, made copies of the picture, attached one to the poem, now on fancy paper. I put the paper in a frame and gave it to him one Christmas, thus turning an extended metaphor into a gift poem. Recently, Brian and his wife had their first child. I revised the poem, altered the title, kept the extended metaphor but redirected the final stanza to suggest that Brian have the same wonderful experiences now with his son (see Figure 8–1).

Working with the Image

Perhaps figurative language is the highest form of language that we can use because it may be the hardest to use. It relies on the use of an image, and all images reside in two worlds, the human world and the natural world. Using figurative language asks us to understand our own world and to connect it to the world of nature. Robert Bly, in his talk "The Six Powers of Poetry," addresses the ways that the image, the fundamental building block, particularly of poetry, brings these worlds together. He points to images in Shakespeare, linked by *of*, such as "a sea of troubles." He suggests that "taking arms against a sea of troubles"

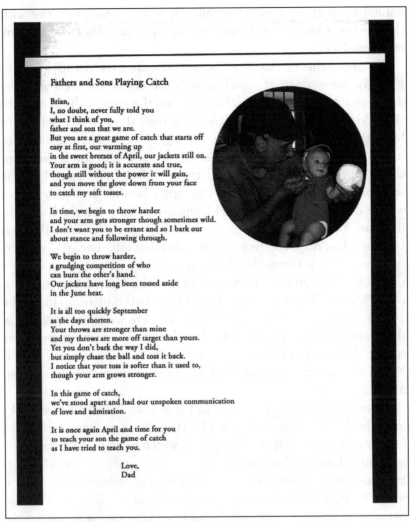

Fathers and Sons Playing Catch

Brian,
I, no doubt, never fully told you
what I think of you,
father and son that we are.
But you are a great game of catch that starts off
easy at first, our warming up
in the sweet breezes of April, our jackets still on.
Your arm is good; it is accurate and true,
though still without the power it will gain,
and you move the glove down from your face
to catch my soft tosses.

In time, we begin to throw harder
and your arm gets stronger though sometimes wild.
I don't want you to be errant and so I bark out
about stance and following through.

We begin to throw harder,
a grudging competition of who
can burn the other's hand.
Our jackets have long been tossed aside
in the June heat.

It is all too quickly September
as the days shorten.
Your throws are stronger than mine
and my throws are more off target than yours.
Yet you don't bark the way I did,
but simply chase the ball and toss it back.
I notice that your toss is softer than it used to,
though your arm grows stronger.

In this game of catch,
we've stood apart and had our unspoken communication
of love and admiration.

It is once again April and time for you
to teach your son the game of catch
as I have tried to teach you.

Love,
Dad

Figure 8–1 "Fathers and Sons Playing Catch"

is very different from facing your problems. Bly argues that it is the sea of troubles that links the very human word *trouble* with the word *sea*, which is not only not human but it takes us into the natural world where the sea is so large. The image takes us away from remaining in the human world. Images seem to force us out of our own little world and help us to touch nature. This living in two worlds doesn't seem natural to most students. Generally, they are coming to terms with their own self-identity and don't venture out when they come to think of themselves.

Bly also believes that the image connects us vertically, that is, joins the known part of ourselves with the unknown, even with the dream or subconscious world. He adds that the image calls us out into the wild, away from our tame lives. It is the call to go somewhere, to leave the protected area. Finally, Bly suggests that the image calls us into the power of analogy, an idea that he got from the Englishman Owen Barfield in his book *Poetic Diction* (1984). Bly expains how the word *analogy* contains the word *logic* and when we deal with images we are connecting with implied comparisons in the logical area. To illustrate Barfield's point, Bly quotes a short poem by Yeats that has become a favorite over the years. It seems that after twenty-five years of loving Maude Gonne but being rejected by her, Yeats received a telegram, while giving a poetry reading in the United States, which read, "Maude Gonne married Major McBride last night." Though he was devastated, his friends suggested that there were plenty of fish in the ocean and that they would help him out. They arranged to have a little dinner each Friday night and invite a young woman over. If Yeats liked her, then he could ask her to marry him and forget about Maude.

After the first dinner, he said to his friends, "She's nice; should I marry her?" This went on for a few Friday nights and, around this time, he wrote the poem called "Memory," in which he states that the lovely faces and charm of these women were in vain and didn't make a last-ing impression on him the way Maude had. Yeats doesn't state the rea-son in those words but rather in an analogy, saying that the presence of the mountain hare cannot help but have a lasting impression on the mountain grass by leaving its form.

Bly contends that metaphors that say she left her mark on him are flat and uninteresting. The task is to describe the reality of Yeats' life in which he felt committed to Maude. Instead, Yeats gives us the image of a place in the mountain where the grass is all knocked down into a little swirl because a rabbit had slept there the night before. Once that swirl is made, it takes more than just a couple of Friday nights for it to leave. The image receives its power because the rabbit isn't there but the swirl remains. Bly offers that the image reveals the major difference between Yeats and Maude Gonne, one that Barfield would read as a series of logical equivalents in the form of an analogy: A is to B as C is to D. Bly suggests that the reader can insert some of his own comparisons and he gives us a few of his own: "The nest of grass is to the hare as form is to what fills it," suggesting it is a poem about form in a way. Another is this: "the mountain grass is to the hare as my receptive psyche is to your wild energy." Barfield holds that an image contains those series of ratios and Bly adds that making one of those images demonstrates great intelligence. Bly contends that the images in Shakespeare's works have some of the highest levels of intelligence and concludes by saying that Yeats has said a tremendous amount in a few words by his use of the image.

Getting students to participate in the form of language is difficult at first, but they can be walked through some of this metaphorical thinking, particularly when it is close to home. I ask them to examine their own writing habits and patterns, asking them a series of questions about the times, places, and manner in which they write best and worst. We then think of the patterns as either hurried or slow and deliberate, gushing or raging with power, trickling or flowing like the inevitable tides. I give them starters such as "When I write (or when my writing is going well) I am like ... ," and ask them to fill in a series of elements from nature such as a wild bull, out of control, or a raging river, rushing to its destiny. They can be as steady as the rolling tide or as relentless as a middle linebacker. There are limitless possibilities for comparison. The trick is to sustain these similes by looking at other characteristics of the natural element to see how they can be associated with other aspects of the writing process, whether it is revising, publishing, working at collecting images in a writer's notebook, or any other stage. Students can then begin to play with making the leap to the metaphor when they drop the words *like* or *as* and say, "I am a garden of ideas with blooms coming year round because of the cultivation I provide for my writing." The writer could then use different pieces for the different kinds of flowers, each with its own fragrance and texture. Again, the possibilities are endless but the exercise stretches the minds of students to see beyond their own human condition. It takes them into the natural world for a while, an uncommon habitat for most teenagers.

More Extended Metaphors in Prose

Jeanine wrote the following prose piece as an extended metaphor and included it in her portfolio under the category of students examining themselves as writers.

Reflection of Myself as a Writer

I am the sun. I wake up and rise above the horizon with each new piece. Creatures gather and life begins all around for me to observe. From a distance I watch people together, from tiny children to elderly couples. I add them to my list of possible topics. I move across the sky with great anticipation of what these ideas will bring. Slowly, diligently, I craft each word. All the hard work and dedication toward a goal of satisfaction. I hope for admiration, for people to sit and enjoy the glow of each ray, each poem.

I nurture birds of inspiration with my careful caress of light. With each day, the buds will blossom, yielding gardens of poems, stories, and other creations. Some days I am prevented from writing. I hide behind a cover of rain and dismal clouds. In those times I envision my next journey across the sky with a new thought.

As each day draws to a close, and my light drowsily dims as I make my way past the skyline, I prepare for the morning. I contemplate working on the piece to completion, perfecting every flaw, developing the plot, or beginning anew with the sunrise.

Jeanine's portfolio was called *Eternal Sunrise* and this extended metaphor helped her to continue the theme that she set up with her cover picture of the sun beginning to rise on a lighthouse on Montauk, the eastern tip of Long Island. She includes a quote from the naturalist John Muir, who suggested that the grand show of sunrises and sunsets is perpetual, because somewhere in the world there's a sunrise and a sunset occurring.

Jeanine continues this theme in her Dear Reader Letter, which introduced her portfolio.

Dear Reader,

Good morning, good day, good evening, whichever you prefer because "it is always sunrise somewhere; the dew is never all dried at once. . . .

Eternal sunrise, eternal sunset, eternal dawn and gloaming . . . each in its turn as the round earth rolls."

As you read through this portfolio, please keep in mind a theme of rebirth. *Eternal Sunrise* signifies that each piece is unique, just as the sunrise signifies a new beginning to each day. I feel that when I am working on a piece for the time that it takes to reach the finished product, I have the option of putting it aside and starting on a new poem or story. This (along with the idea that no piece is ever complete, that you can never finish revising) helped me to decide that I should name this Eternal Sunrise because I am always able to begin again.

Many long hours have brought me this finished product. Hours of writing individual pieces, poems or prose. Time spent sorting through magazines (such as *National Geographic*, a portfolio maker's best friend) for pictures and family albums for photographs. Then the final hours of selecting which pieces to include, reflecting on them individually and compiling the book itself.

To you, the reader, I extend the warmest of welcomes. I hope that my efforts have not been in vain and that in some way this book leaves an impression on you. Now without further ado, I invite you to experience my writing.

Enjoy!

Jeanine Beatty

It is no wonder that Jeanine would write the extended metaphor of herself as the sun. The idea of continuity has seized her. She begins to live and breathe this concept, and she sees all things as perpetually in motion; she is a part of the moving universe, taking power from it and giving energy back to it. Her portfolio is one example of the creating act that the sun produces. She knows also that this product represents a theme of rebirth and that she is always revising, that no piece is ever fully finished. I met her several times while she was in college and, while she still had a fondness for her portfolio, she told me how she continued to grow as a writer and how she would even revise some of the pieces in her portfolio. However, the act of reflecting on herself then as a writer helped her make the connection between the creative power of the sun and her own creative energy.

As another example, Keri, an eighth grader, put her reflection of herself as a writer into poetry.

Myself as a Writer
As I write, my writing is like the wind blowing through
the leaves on a tree.
The wind is the endless thoughts that keep going.
As it blows through the leaves, it collects thoughts
and leaves with it.
When the wind dies down, thoughts are not collected
but left behind.
Unable to open a new passage between the branches,
my brain almost goes blank.
When my thoughts come back, they are put together as one,
to form a poem, a story, or a prose piece.

—*Keri LaSalla*

Jenn, an eleventh-grade honors student and a superior athlete, played field hockey and basketball and won acclaim and eventually a scholarship as a softball player. In an extended metaphor, she personified her bat as the famous Louisville Slugger type. Then taking on the identity of the bat, she portrayed her struggles in life as a Louisville Slugger.

Louisville Slugger
Dragging my bat through the dirt
up to the plate,
I am unsure of
what lies before me
in this game of life.
Tightly gripping
the soft, black handle,
I prepare myself
for the first inning.

My power will take me
the distance needed
to hit the long ball
or the base hit
with two down
in the bottom of the seventh.

I have a range
of different aspects in my life,
one large enough
to cover the entire strike zone.
But my hard interior
is what will make me reliable
and dependable
deep into the future.

—*Jenn McCaffrey*

Alan, an outstanding eleventh grader, wrote the following extended metaphor that "depicts a supposed battle between the granite cliffs which face each other (El Capitan and Half Dome) in Yosemite Valley, California."

A Test of Time
Wrinkled granite faces stare resolutely at each other,
Immutable feeling of detachment,
Formed by the great schism centuries ago,
Crestless waves frozen in time,
Each waiting for the other
To tumble into the earth.

Crowds gaze up at the epic battle—
Hastening from the foot of one to the other,
They admire the chiseled rock bodies of time,
Snapping photographs of the two,
And the streams of moisture pouring down their faces.

Time passes perpetually,
But minutes are inconsequential
In the indefatigable eternity of geology.
But the foes remain,
Silently belligerent.

—*Alan Lemley*

In his final portfolio, Alan wrote a reflection that included these comments:

Although I had never been to Yosemite Valley, I knew what to expect from the back and white photographs of Ansel Adams (The photograph on the cover of this portfolio is taken from one of his calendars, which my mom buys every year.) A winding half-hour drive brought us into the valley; it was the most thrilling spectacle I've ever witnessed. While words cannot do justice to Yosemite, I felt that I could create an interesting poem by personifying the two most famous cliffs, Half Dome and El Capitan as fighters in a magnificent battle. I thought my poem resembled the strange picture of the statues in the field which I recently discovered on the cover of a Pink Floyd CD. I felt that my poem was well written, but I was worried that readers would not understand my line of thought (the streams of moisture are references to the waterfalls that pour over various spots of the granite cliffs). For this reason, I added the short description which appears before the poem; I also hope the cover photo enhances the poem. (El Capitan is in the left foreground while Half Dome is in the background on the right.) Yosemite Valley is breathtaking—I can only imagine what it is like for those crazy enough to scale the cliffs using ropes and pitons, instead of remaining content to snap photographs from the valley floor.

In the next chapter, we present other ways to involve students in writing extended metaphors.

9

More Extended Metaphors

Jerry Matovcik

To start a unit on writing extended metaphors, I distribute a packet
with the assignment on the cover page, samples of extended metaphors
by professional poets and student poets on the other pages, and a closing page with a list of prompts. The assignment reads as follows:

> Use an extended metaphor to describe your relationship with another
> person (or to describe yourself in relation to others and the world).
> Examine the models in the packet to get an idea of how these
> metaphors work. Use one of the prompts from the last page or invent
> your own to get you started. Your poem should be at least twelve lines.

I start with an earlier version of Jim's revised poem called, "Fathers
and Sons Playing Catch" (see Chapter 8), a poem students enjoy
because they can identify with the activity. After all, throwing a baseball back and forth is an apt American metaphor for the lasting connections and temporary contentions between a father and son. The
pastoral setting with its cycle of changing seasons as a metaphor for our
human seasons of youth, maturity, and old age are archetypal elements
that make the poem very appealing. As mentioned earlier, we suggest
students begin their poems with the phrase, "You are . . ." and then
launch into their extended metaphor. Jim introduces the extended
metaphor phrase in his poem by speaking to Brian first as father to son:
"you are a game of catch." Challenging students to invent unique
introductions might help in getting the poems to sound less standardized and formulaic. Students will want to try their hand at it.

Next we read and discuss the other samples from professional poets and student writers. Some of the poems are "Mother to Son" by Langston Hughes, "Mushrooms" and "You're" by Sylvia Plath, "It Dropped So Low in My Regard" by Emily Dickinson, "When She Was Here, Li Bo, She Was Like Cold Summer Lager" by Peter Williams, "A Noiseless Patient Spider" by Walt Whitman, and "A Simile for Her Smile" by Richard Wilbur. After reading and discussing these poems and those by former students, I refer to a list of prompts to help get students started. (See Figure 9–1.) For some students who are really stuck, a prompt from the list gets them started. Most students, however, take the list as a challenge to be playful and invent their own extended metaphor, since it is obvious from the variety of prompts that any metaphor can work if it's logical and intelligent. Topics such as "You Are a Sea Otter," "Life Is an Egg," "You Are a Leaf Fluttering in the Wind," and "You Are a Siamese Cat" suddenly begin to emerge.

I always look forward to reading the extended metaphors my students have written because of the surprising and clever analogies they use to describe relationships. The following are some student poems that I use as models. In his poem, "Solar Flares," Alex, an eleventh grader, demonstrates that he has been paying attention in his astronomy class and found an apt way to express his attraction to a member of the opposite sex.

Solar Flares
You are the little flame that bounces back and forth;
Playful, you don't know your power.
Maybe you're more like the sun in my eyes,
Distracting when I look at you, yet my gaze always
returns to your radiant aura.

Your air is the vast darkness that sweeps the night sky
as it sweeps your face.
Comets of tears may streak your cheeks
Only to make you glow brighter;
A luminous light-generator
That powers dim rooms and dark halls.

You are planetary, a heavenly body,
Always out of my strained reaches.
Elliptical in your travels, a twisty winding,

You are a crystal plate on my top shelf.

You are a home full of warm rooms.

You are a melody.

You are a red, red rose.

You are a rocking chair.

You are a cedar cabinet.

You are a quilt of many patterns.

You are a rainbow.

You are a thunderstorm.

You are a rich jewel.

You are a sparkling stream.

You are the waves of the ocean.

You are a flowing river.

You are a kaleidoscope.

You are a crossword puzzle.

You are a bouquet of fresh flowers.

You are a cold lager in summer.

You are a box turtle, steady and determined.

You are a palette of colors.

You are a new minted coin.

You are a wild colt.

You are a sparkling soda.

You are a morning fog.

You are a tennis match.

You are a horse-shoe well struck.

You are a new window.

You are a mountain climber.

You are a game of football.

Figure 9–1 Extended Metaphor Prompts

You tilt on your axis about me,
But never close enough to embrace,
Though I can feel your gravity pull me.

Perhaps I should forget you.
(How can I recall something so far away?)
But, alas, I have only hope
Springing from my fiery depths,
Hope that one day your orbit will cross mine.

—*Alex Deturk*

In his circular poem about a cup of coffee, Eric's sense of humor is at play as he describes how he tries to rekindle a relationship that has quickly gone cold with some sweet words and half-truths.

Coffee: Can't Live with It; Can't Live Without It
You're a scalding hot cup of coffee,
Badly needed to satiate my addiction,
Yet you're the cause of these sublime headaches.
At first dark, brooding, even headstrong,
But I give you a little sugar,
Half 'n Half of reality,
And you've lightened up, sweetened to my lips.
Bold and smooth,
I can't help but drink you up.
Of course, if I'm not paying attention,
You grow cold just like *that*.
Oh, I'll try to cut back,
Try to swear off of you for good,
But . . .

—*Eric Gottlieb*

In the next poem, candy becomes an analogue for the tantalizing sweetness of a relationship. As I read the poem, I have to admire Brianna's smart choice of the various terms and ideas that extend the analogy. The poem itself becomes a real "treat" that rewards readers and lingers in our imagination.

After Taste
You are the lasting taste of candy,
Pleasant and sweet.

Even when our time together fades
And your presence slowly dissolves,
Your endless sensation remains,
Lingering on my lips.
Your ever-lasting flavor,
Now only a bitter-sweet reminder of what once was,
Leaves me craving for another piece,
Another chance.
Our experience now just a past treat.
I can only savor the sense of you,
Which rests upon my tongue.
You are the lasting taste of candy—
Just as potent when gone.

—*Brianna Rasmuson*

Of course, not every relationship is so sweet; so a teenage writer turns to other analogies to convey her experience. From time to time, a student produces a poem that transcends the simple requirements of the assignment, and the metaphor matches the complexity of a relationship. In a poem, "Upkeep and Spring," Valerie Rose Nutt describes the reciprocal nourishment and disappointment experienced in a relationship in terms of a gardener attentive to her plants. The gardener waters her plant with comforting life, only to find that the plant goes dry and needs constant upkeep. In turn, the plant, a cherubic pansy, breaks through the "frosting sadness" of the gardener in the spring, but as summer progresses, the plant withdraws and leaves the gardener with a cold heart. The poem is about trying to penetrate the mystery of another person, as though what we first see of the other is only the superficial, muted grays of twilight. The true eyes of a relationship can penetrate the twilight and see the hues beneath the dark.

Writing Techniques: The Juxtaposition of Images and the Use of the Word *Of*

Valerie's poem raises the bar and gives other young writers something to aim for. Since Jim and I like to use student examples to teach effective writing techniques, I use Valerie's poem to teach metaphorical writing through the juxtaposition of images. Some metaphors are born through the juxtaposition of two apparently dis-similar things. Put images side by side, and a reader is compelled to see the likenesses and connections. A classic example of this is Ezra Pound's "In a Station of the Metro," a poem of two lines in which the appearance of faces of a crowd in a Paris subway is followed by the line, "Petals on a wet, black bough." The nameless faces that materialize in the silence of that dark, damp subterranean world are captured in the concrete image of the bough. Valerie uses the same technique in her poem in the line, "I wonder, how deep does it get? Watching intent the tiny droplets, perfect pilgrims wayfaring to your base." The apposition of the image "perfect pilgrims" with the phrase "tiny droplets" suggests that the nourishing attention of the narrator in the poem is a form of religious devotion, that the jour-ney to the depths of another person is as long and gratifying as a pil-grimage to a holy shrine. One recalls Romeo's line to Juliet, "My lips, two blushing pilgrims, ready stand."

In his book, *Teaching Poetry Writing to Adolescents,* Joseph Tsujimoto (1996) uses a similar approach to introduce his middle-school students to metaphorical thinking and writing. His students write two-word poems, in which they juxtapose two concrete nouns, and the juxtapo-sition charges the words with several layers of meaning. In engaging exercises that can be used on any grade level, Tsujimoto encourages further metaphorical thinking through word association games and the writing of circle poems and transformation poems.

I also foster metaphorical writing through another technique: the use of the word *of* in an analogy to join unlike things and suggest their sim-ilarity. I point out the famous examples from Shakespeare in which the prince of Denmark bears the "slings and arrows *of* outrageous fortune" or Richard III claims, "Now is the winter *of* our discontent made glorious summer by this son of York." We also have Alonzo's remark to Gonzalo in *The Tempest,* "You cram these words in mine ears against the stomach *of* my sense." In these images, Shakespeare combines a concrete noun with an abstract one with the denotation of each word carrying sugges-tive meaning for other. So the expression "winter of our discontent" con-nects the great unhappiness with the overwhelming cold of winter. After examining this technique, student writers create their own metaphorical images by combining concrete and abstract nouns or two concrete nouns. We have seen some of this imagery in the sample student poems in this chapter: "comets of tears" from "Solar Flares"; and "Half 'n Half of reality" from "Coffee: Can't Live with It; Can't Live Without It." In other metaphorical poems, one student described a stormy relationship with the phrases "a vortex of spinning emotions" and "a tidal wave of tears." Another student described the watering of a flowering relationship as "a delicate dribble of comforting life."

A Special Insight

After I assign writing a particular form of poetry like the extended metaphor, I like to get the students started in the computer lab so they can work under my supervision. I remind students to start writing and get some words and ideas down without being overly self-critical, and in the very process, to expect the unexpected. Writing becomes a process of uncovering ideas and materials one did not anticipate, like clearing a garden in spring only to find the young sprouts have already germinated on their own. I also find that by circulating in the computer lab and saying, "Show me what's working," or "Show me what you are having a hard time with," I can help keep the students' writing process flowing.

If a student is stuck in writer's block, I ask the class to help the student brainstorm more ideas for the extended metaphor so the student can set sail again on the writing task. If a student writes, "You are a new-minted coin" and draws a blank, I ask the class to brainstorm about new coins. They might respond: "they are shiny," "they stand out from old coins," "they jingle in your pocket," or "they are saved and collected." The student writer now will have more material to work with, and eventually, over a number of days, a poem may be struck.

In writing extended metaphors, students begin to sense the power that comes with the art of writing. They also learn that writing as an art contains a good deal of artifice, witty ingenuity, and clever delivery. Some students think that their extended metaphors about relationships are exaggerated truths or total fictions, but upon examination, they realize that they have come closer to the truth for all readers than they first thought. They begin to recognize the value of stretching the images in their writing, leading to greater appreciation for the writing of others and a greater sense of confidence in their own ability to extend metaphors.

Write Before Their Eyes
On Nature Poems

Jerry Matovcik

When I introduce my unit on writing nature poems, I give my students a little aural quiz first. I ask, "What bird makes this sound: *'Drink your tea . . . Drink your tea'?*" The students look puzzled. "A British bird," one student quips, but no one can name the bird. So I tell the class that it is the "rufous-sided towhee." There are some snickers and laughs. "What does 'rufous' mean?" someone calls out. Then I explain that these birds are common in our area, and are probably in our own back-yards if we paid attention. The rufous-sided towhee, a bird with a black head, neck and shoulders, a white chest, and rust-red (rufous) wings and sides, is a sociable bird who likes to be watched by humans as he scavenges through leaves on the forest floor for insects. My next aural question is, "Which bird makes this sound: *'Teakettle . . . tea-kettle . . . teakettle'?*" "Birds really like 'tea,'" someone chimes in, but again, most students are stumped. "It's a Carolina wren," I tell the class. Then I describe this chunky, rusty-brown bird with the uplifted tail, only now some students claim they have actually seen this bird at their bird-feeders. The last aural question in my nature quiz is "Who makes this call: *'Bob-white . . . Bob-white'?*" The students are stumped again so I tell them it is the Northern Bobwhite, a reddish-brown quail named after his own call. I have seen a covey of these birds, walking in a row across my driveway. The purpose of my aural quiz is to alert students to the fact that they will miss the natural world all around them if they do not learn to be attentive. (At some point, I will read to them Mary Oliver's poem, "Two Mockingbirds," about being attentive to nature and receiving blessings in return.) But for now, I want to get the students outside so they can see what they are missing.

After my brief lesson in bird calls, I ask my students to take their notebooks and a pen, and we go out the back door to the back field, in ways similar to Jim's account in Chapter 2. Since our approaches are different in some ways, perhaps the journey bears retelling for the variations. At the far end of the field, I notice some movement on the grass, and point it out to my students. Some of them with good eyesight notice three birds, darting across the field, stopping, then running off again. My student Matt, with the best eyes, notices that the birds have distinct double black bands on their white breasts. I point out to the students that these are killdeer, a kind of plover or shore bird that commonly stops over in fields. When we pass the field and go into the woods behind the school, we see a chipmunk eating an acorn, and everyone remarks about how cute the little critter looks. Along the path in the woods, we see a tiny spider absolutely still in her gossamer web. Farther on, someone spies a gray tree frog stuck Spiderman-like to the side of a fence post. Another student notices a small section of charred, bare trees with new growth at their base, and many recall the fire in the woods over a year ago.

In class the next day, after rehearsing ideas in my mind, I write the following poem on the blackboard off the top of my head and before the students' eyes. The main idea came to me after our short field trip behind the high school that all creatures, no matter their size, have to eat. I tell students that I have taken notes, just as they did, and I will create four stanzas, each one showing one or more of those creatures looking for food. That will be my organization. Each stanza will start by identifying a place along our walk. From there, I write and talk.

Morning Meals
Out on the back field, three killdeer
Dart across the grass, looking for insects,
Their brown bodies blending with the brown grass,
Camouflage, a moving mirage.

In the woods, a brown blur
Streaks from under dark leaves—
A chipmunk, on his haunches,
Munching the meat of an acorn,
Holding the acorn cup in his miniscule hands.

Along the path, a tiny spider
With legs as thin as an eyelash,

Feels the filaments of her web
For the vibration of a fine repast.

Back in the cafeteria, students queue up,
Their eyes darting, their feet vibrating,
Their stomachs feeling for food,
Hoping to bag a bagel for breakfast.

As I am writing the poem before their eyes, I point out that I chose the word *blend* in the first stanza because it sounded best with the alliteration of "brown bodies." Because we could not see the killdeer at first, I described them as a "moving mirage," and the word *camouflage* just came to me because its rhymes with *mirage* and expresses how the birds' colors conceal them. I also explain how I first saw the chipmunk as a blur because chipmunks move so quickly on the ground. Why did I decide on the word *munching*? I picked the word because it echoes the -*munk* in chipmunk and alliterates with the rest of the line.

At this point in the poem, at the third stanza, I tell students that prepositional phrases have now surfaced for me as organizational cues for my experiences. "Out on the soccer field," "In the woods," these initial phrases give coherence to the order and place of what I had seen that morning. Logically then, I start my third stanza with "Along the path," and my final stanza with, "Back in the cafeteria." Alliteration seems to be working for me as well. "Feels the filament . . . of a fine repast" and "bag a bagel" seem to arise for me as I am crafting my poem.

When I am done writing my poem on the board, I ask the students for a title. Since I had so much alliteration in the poem, one of my ninth graders suggests "Morning Meals." I like the title, so I write it above the poem.

So here you have a poem that I wrote before the students' eyes after a walk outside with them, a poem that came from being attentive to the natural world around us.

10

Getting Outside

Poems About Nature

Jerry Matovcik

> Reedy monotones of locust, or sounds of katydid—I hear the
> latter at night, and the other both day and night. I thought the
> morning and evening warble of birds delightful; but I find I can
> listen to these strange insects with just as much pleasure.
>
> —Walt Whitman, *Specimen Days*

Early in my teaching career, Walt Whitman taught me to get outside. Reading the catalogues of animals, insects, and wildflowers from Whitman's *Leaves of Grass* would energize me, reminding me of my connection to the natural world. After reading passages of the poem, I would often feel a desire to walk where the mockingbird mimics the rich musical phrases of other birds, where the hummingbird sips nectar from a flower, where the long-necked swan glides by the rushes of a creek, and where the yellow-crowned night-heron walks along mudflats foraging for food (Whitman 1982, 61). Whitman, an astute naturalist, even later in life as he recuperated in New Jersey from his paralytic stroke, would spend summers in the "primitive solitude" of Timber Creek, enjoying all the charms of nature, recounting these sojourns in *Specimen Days*. The more I read of Whitman's poetry and prose, the memories of Long Island beaches and marshes, and of boyhood adventures on the Great South Bay woven through *Leaves of Grass*, the more I felt compelled to get outside and, like Whitman, go on foot "absorbing" fields, sea, and shore. What better opportunity could my students and I have, living on Long Island, Whitman's beloved "Paumanok." Perhaps, in our own small way, we could, like the Good Gray Poet, contain the natural world around us in words; we too could "contain multitudes."

Some years ago, I arranged a field trip to Quogue Wildlife Refuge on the south fork of Long Island where a volunteer naturalist gave us a tour of the refuge, educating us on the Latin as well as the common names of the various plants, bushes, and trees found there. We spotted several painted turtles basking on the limb of tree that had fallen over a stream. We learned what sphagnum moss looked like and how a pine forest regenerated itself after a brush fire. We examined an injured golden eagle that park rangers at the center were nursing back to health. My ninth-grade students took copious notes.

When we returned to the classroom the following week, we wrote catalogue poems that listed all that we saw on our day outdoors. I recall now that on the way home from the wildlife refuge that afternoon, my students asked me if we could stop at the beach, so I had the bus driver make an unscheduled stop, now almost impossible after 9/11. My students and I took off our shoes and socks, rolled up our jeans, and waded into the water, just as Whitman had done so many years earlier when he grew up on Long Island. Whitman loved to float on the soft waves in "the billowy drowse" of the sea. So, I advise, get outdoors with your students and see what surprises nature has to offer.

Why Nature Poems?

The purpose of teaching a unit on nature poems is not just to write poems or pass standardized tests, but to teach students that we are part of the larger order of things. In doing this, we hope they will take a stance toward nature that is one of distance, wonder, appreciation, and even celebration. This stance toward nature is rendered very powerfully by Theodore Roethke in his poem, "Moss-Gathering," whose narrator pulls up patches of moss to decorate baskets and other plants sold at the nursery, yet he feels terrible about tearing the moss out of the earth. We hope to teach students to observe the natural world and its ecosystems, fostering a respect for the diversity of life and encouraging a thoughtful stewardship of the lands and waters around us.

Writing Catalogue Poems

When you cannot arrange a field trip for your students, at least draw on their experiences outdoors. Here is the easiest way to get students to write catalogue poems, or poems that list activities students participate in when they are outside. First, the teacher can make copies of the lists or catalogues from Walt Whitman's *Leaves of Grass*, in particular, sections 14 and 33 from "Song of Myself," and his poem "I Hear America Singing." To warm up to the writing, have all the students in the class stand next to their desks, and then go down the rows, having each student read a verse aloud in the robust voice of someone walking outdoors on an exhilarating day. You want students to feel the incantatory rhythms that are created by the repetition, parallel structure, and the enumeration of images. They should have a sense that they are reciting a prayer in a robust voice or a chant.

When students are finished reciting, discuss Whitman's style. I point out several rhetorical devices that Whitman uses: *anaphora* (the repetition of same word or words at the beginning of a line), *alliteration, assonance* and *consonance, rhetorical questions,* and *commands*. The overall effect of all these elements in a catalogue of long lines is almost spiritual. Whitman's lists, which contain disparate events and experiences happening simultaneously, give the poem a feeling of timelessness and solidarity, as though all beings are eternally connected.

To convey this sense of connectedness, the class writes a long catalogue poem, with each student contributing a stanza. The following are the steps of the assignment, followed by an example of my writing.

Class Catalogue Poem
1. Write for five minutes in prose, describing an activity you do outdoors—fishing, biking, gardening, hiking, and so on.
2. Write in the present tense, putting the reader "there" as you are doing the activity. Don't tell us, "I'm fishing." Instead, show us what is happening.
3. Use Whitman's long lines and rhetorical devices (see next section) to create a sense of the enormity of the motion in the universe with the circling of the planets and the pull of the moon on the tides.

Whitman's Devices
Rhetorical Question: Has anyone supposed it lucky to be born?

First Person: I am of old and young, of the foolish as much as the wise.

Bold Statement: I am the poet of the Body and I am the poet of the Soul.

Direct Address: You sea! I resign myself to you also—I guess what you mean.

Imperative Voice: Listen, I will be honest with you.

Address the Reader: (Is it night? Are we here alone?)

Exclamation: Ah, what can be more stately and admirable to me than masthemm'd Manhattan!

My Prose Version (about crabbing)

I am crabbing on a summer night. The moon is shining and lighting up the water. The peaceful sound of the waves is hypnotizing me. I'm looking for crabs with a flashlight. When I see a crab, I get all excited. But when I pull him up, I realize the water magnified him double in size.

My Poetic Version (using some of Whitman's devices)

Have you ever waited for a crab on a beautiful summer night? (Rhetorical Question)

The moon is shining bright as a spotlight.

The peaceful lapping of the waves against the boat hypnotizes me.

Look! There he is! A portly gentleman scurrying off for an important date. (Exclamation)

I snatch him in my net, eager to brag about so enormous a catch. (Bold Statement)

I pull him into the open air only to discover that the water magnified the scrawny creature twice his actual size!

After my initial instructions and direction, my students produced a very long class catalogue poem that captured the energy of their outdoor experiences. Here are some stanzas from that poem, each stanza by a combination of students.

I am skateboarding down my block, pushing as hard and as fast as I
can with my right foot.
As I crouch down to grab my board, I stare at the wooden launch ramp.
When I make contact with the ramp, I fly through the air, the blood
rushes to my head.
When I land, I could hear my friends cheer.

I shun long periods in the sun, so I bicycle at night.
The seat is small and lightly padded, making it uncomfortable, but I
don't care.

Elbows locked, hands gripping savagely tight, with my head tilted
    forward,
I inspect the road in front of me for potholes that are difficult to see in
    the dark.
Legs pumping, radio blasting, I cut through the night.
The more I sweat, the better!

The early bird *does* catch the worm!
At five-thirty A.M., while my friends sleep and dream, I stalk the yard
    for bait.
The morning mist is as soft and quiet as a mother tip-toeing into her
    child's room.
At the far corner of a clearing, I pierce the ground with my small
    spade; the blade slides cleanly in,
And the pungent aroma of earth penetrates my nostrils.
I have done this enough to know that as soon as I turn the dirt, a riot
    of worms will twist and curl and run for cover.

In January, I slide in my boots across the ice at the beach.
I soar sideways where the sand used to be.
My laughter sparkles just like the dazzle of a thousand tiny lights from
    the sun on the frigid waves.

I pull the delicate stem from the pot, the fragile net of roots holds the
    loam as I plant my flower.
I mix and match the vibrant colors and admire them as I go along.
I am reminded by the scent of peat moss and fresh air that summer is
    near.

Seeing

In her book *Pilgrim at Tinker Creek*, a meditation on appreciating the
natural world, Annie Dillard (1974) has a wonderful chapter on *seeing*.
As a little girl, Dillard would plant pennies in her neighborhood so
some passersby would discover one of the shiny coins and think they
had received a free gift from the universe. She would draw arrows with
a sign "surprise ahead" or "money this way" so the coins would be discovered. Dillard goes on to explain that nature, like this little girl, casts
innumerable pennies for us to experience if we have the disposition to
follow the arrows, if we have the eyes to see. One of the reasons we

have students write nature poems is to alert them to the arrows and accustom their eyes to see the gifts of wonder and free surprises that nature sends.

How does one learn to see? How does one learn what to look for? One could arrange a field trip to a local park, wildlife refuge, or nature conservancy, and draw on the expertise of a professional guide. For a fee, park rangers will visit your classroom, bringing animals. Teachers can also find books in the local library with pictures and descriptions of local flora and fauna that can be photocopied and distributed to a class. The Internet, of course, contains extensive resources. You can start by searching for "nature conservancy" to find your local chapter. Type in "wolf spider" on your search engine, and you will receive your first easy and informative lessons on the natural world. The Discovery Channel is another great resource. I once met a student who knew everything there is to know about sharks, and he said he learned it on the Discovery Channel. But, most of all, I encourage you to take nature walks and guided tours yourself. Local libraries offer them, and of course, local nature groups, too. In a short period of time, you will become very knowledgeable, and you will be able to see many treasures you overlooked before.

The simplest place to introduce students to writing about the outdoors is on the school grounds or in any wooded property around the school. On a beautiful day in the fall, I would ask students to take their writer's notebook and follow me out the back door of the school to see what we could see. On the way, someone might stir up a grasshopper or notice the imprint of shoes on the muddy ground. Students begin to bend and crouch lower to observe. At the edge of a field, I point to the sheen of dew drops on the silken tent of a wolf spider. We go through the fence and down a path in the woods. One of my students who knows a little about nature tells us about the three different shapes of leaves on a sassafras tree. Someone notices the lichen on the bark of some oaks. Another sees a cavity in the bole of a tree, a suitable home for chipmunks or field mice. Others point at debris left behind, a tossed Gatorade bottle or an empty box of cigarettes. A snake slithers from under some wet leaves, and some students scream while others want to pick it up. I don't think a teacher has to be a naturalist to take students outside to observe. In my experience, the students notice enough to make the simple journey rewarding.

The next step is to encourage students to get outdoors themselves and practice more direct observation, selecting something from the environment that impresses them, or moves them emotionally. I model the idea that any object rightly regarded can display its special signature with the poems "Young Sycamore" by William Carlos Williams, "The Willows of Massachusetts" by Denise Levertov, "Nomad Exquisite" by Wallace Stevens, and two prose poems by Robert Bly. In typical imagist style, Williams describes, in a single sentence, a young sycamore rising out of the gutter of a city street. In a similar way, Levertov praises the endurance of willow trees "last to relinquish leaf" in the cold of winter. Stevens sings a single periodic sentence hymn of praise celebrating the lush native vegetation of Florida. Robert Bly turns his imaginative powers to "Looking at a Dead Wren in My Hand" and "A Turtle." Together, my students and I read these poems, discussing the approaches and techniques of the poets and what they were trying to convey.

What Gifts Did Nature Offer to You?

Whether on a field trip or on a walk of their own, I ask my students to respond to one basic question, what gifts did nature offer to you? I explain that they could take two approaches to developing material for a poem. As a first approach, I tell students to "go with your story," assuming that most would have a story to tell about adventuring out into their neighborhood. The second approach is to encourage students to weave a poem out of the emotions and thoughts evoked by an outdoor experience.

Here are some student poems written in response to nature. The first poem by a tenth grader describes the emotions evoked by an outdoor experience. He transforms his memories of his childhood with his cousin on a farm into a prize-winning poem for the Walt Whitman Poetry Contest.

Running Clear
Hot August on my uncle's farm.
I sit in the loft of the brick red barn,
my feet hanging out of the window,
my hands braced upon the floor.

And out of that loft I see
a small creek, running clear.
My heart leaps.
"Look there," I whisper
as I tug my cousin's arm.

We climb down through the broken hatch,
through the deserted stables, brushing away the webs.
I look up at my cousin, long and lanky.
He is growing up fast.
Still, the slender frame needs to be filled in.
Yet so skilled and smart,
so much what I want to be.

He takes a long rusted knife off the wall
and we head to the creek,
a fantasy world of unfound wonder.

We sprawl through the fence
and scramble to the field.
The sun stretches to its highest,
beating on our backs.
It gives us a renewed purpose,
to quench the heat.

He pulls out the knife
and hacks down the long stalks.
It cuts back at us,
bleeding our ankles, slicing our legs.
I jump up to get a quick peek.
Seeing the creek, I give a shout,
"We're almost there!"

My cousin stomps down the last ten feet,
a rhinoceros trampling the thicket.
We pull back the vines,
and see the white cascade
of running water crashing on the rocks.
We kick off our shoes and peel off our shirts.
Dipping our feet in, we scatter fish.
We wade in the cool knee-deep water,
dunking our heads, bringing the water raining down our backs.

We splash and laugh and take joy in our hidden paradise.

We head back to the house,
tired and happy,
leaving behind a trail of dripping water
that we can follow back to our friendship
as it's found at the ends
of the tunnels of our minds.

—*Jody Shenn*

Jody has taken the image of a creek running clear and has connected it with the desire of young friends who want to run clear in summer joy. He captures the pleasures of a beautiful scene by participating in all of its sensual satisfactions. At the same time, this experience is made even stronger because of the bond of friendship.

Brian, an eleventh grader, records his observations of being on the beach of the Long Island Sound. In the process, he plays with the word *sound* for the song the water gives, for the celebration of this favorite place, and for the various sounds he creates with his use of alliteration.

Summer Song
As I lie on her rocky shore,
Sweet sea music surrounds me.
Her shell filled sands caress me.
Smooth breezes float over,
Carrying the scent of the sea.
Gulls circle, searching,
Swings sway,
Squeaking, singing their song.
Shells collect in hands of little ones,
Each with its own melody.
Salty skins tan slowly,
Clouds gather, dancing together.
Children frolic joyfully,
Laughing as sand plays in their toes.
The tide crashes against the rocky coast,
Creating a symphony of notes.
The sweet Sound pleases all.

—*Brian Walsh*

Writing Techniques—Student Models

Sometimes I encourage students to try new techniques such as repetition or commands. As I conference with students, I often notice how a particular student has captured a trait of a poet we've studied and I ask permission to use that poem in a minilesson the next day in class and in all of my classes. I find it is very powerful to use the work of my students as models for other students. Sometimes the student is present and I ask him or her to explain the technique to the rest of the class. I end by encouraging others to try what this student has done. I find that this works better than any other single approach, because students feel empowered when they see what their peers are capable of writing. The following three poems were written by juniors without the benefit of a field trip. In the first poem, Meghan uses repetition (the first and last line of each stanza, and the repeated verb *shrieks* with the phrase "like a siren's call") to reinforce how she is absorbed or "lost" in her experience.

Down on the Beach
Down on the beach
Where the grass grows tall
And the wind shrieks wildly
Like a siren's call,
The waves overtake me
And set me at ease—
I am no sailor
But I am lost at sea.

Down on a beach
By a cold sand wall
Where the grass shrieks wildly
Like a siren's call,
My fingers go numb
But I'm not ready to leave—
I am no sailor
But I'm lost at sea.

    —*Meghan Callen*

In a poem reminiscent of "After Apple Picking" by Robert Frost (although Danielle had not read it), the writer starts with a command, asking forgiveness for her addiction to apple picking.

Apples
Forgive me!
Walking through the orchard,
My mind spinning, I am tempted by evil.
Fruit that cast man out of Eden.
Expulsion from paradise.
Pain, suffering, hardship,
The destruction of mankind.

Forgive me!
I have thieved from endless rows of trees,
Overfilling buckets, apples spilling over,
Getting dusted by earth.
More than I could ever need,
My selfish addiction,
So wicked, so delicious!

Forgive me
Their seductive nature,
The desired color of lips.
My mouth breaking their skin,
Chewing their white insides.
Frothy juice
Seeping from the corners of my mouth.
Sticky, sweet, intoxicating smell,
What sinful pleasure!

—*Danielle Korshak*

Sonja's nature poem is an occasion to say something about commercialism, but her use of the imperative mood has a subtle sarcastic tone.

Naturally Artificial
O come and sit on this beautiful commercial beach!
Grab a fist full of this bagged sand
And let it slip through your fingers.
Wade in the cerulean-dyed water.
Splash, dive, float!
Oh how delightful to lose yourself in this tamed wilderness!
I think I'll order a drink, or perhaps two.
What do I care, I am in *paradise*.
Do you smell the fragrant jasmine blossoms and the ocean breeze?

You can buy them bottled in the specialty shop across the way.
Do you hear the sound of the tiny, black pebbles as they drag along
    the shore?
You can buy them in a dainty box on a bed of cotton.
Do you see the intensity of the flaming orange sun
And the black silhouette of tropical palms dancing in the wind?
You can capture them forever on laminated postcards at the souvenir
    shop.
O, how exquisitely domestic is our hotel!
Tall and opulent against the open ocean and the velvet cloak of night
    skies.
They shower the night with fast firecrackers
Because stationary stars are so passé.
It's so nice to be in touch with nature.
It's so exhilarating to run free,
To sprint across this powdery beach
And dig my heels into the waves.
Lungs full of oxygen,
Muscles bursting with vitality,
I can be anything or go anywhere
Except—
Well, except beyond that red and white sign
That indicates our share of *paradise.*

—*Sonja Mauro*

There are many kinds of nature poems that could be used as models if you examine a number of anthologies. Poems like "The Bat" by Theodore Roethke, "The Crabs" by Richmond Lattimore, and "Gracious Goodness" by Marge Piercy describe human encounters with creatures from the wild, presented as occasions to say things about survival, virtue, and our kinship with the animal kingdom. "The Bat" is cousin to a mouse and wears a "human face"; "The Crabs" boil in a can for "the good cheer of civilized man"; "Gracious Goodness" finds the poet rescuing a royal tern who had become entangled in a fishing line and hook. Piercy ends the poem with a question that invites the reader into the experience. And I like to read Seamus Heaney's "The Death of a Naturalist" for a lesson on how to laugh at ourselves in our feeble attempts to comprehend the wild landscapes around us.

Urban Kids

What do you do if you're teaching in the city and not in the suburbs of Long Island? My advice would be to arrange field trips to local parks, botanical gardens, and wildlife preserves. For example, the boroughs of Brooklyn and Queens in New York City encompass 2,500 acres of The Jamaica Bay Wildlife Refuge. This refuge, the only one in the national park system, provides a variety of habitats for more than three hundred kinds of waterfowl and shorebirds. It is a critical stop-over area along the Eastern Flyway migration route and is one of the best bird-watching locations in the western hemisphere. New York City's Central Park is also located along this migration route, and the Central Park Conservancy conducts free walking tours and educational programs.

I would also recommend that teachers in urban as well as suburban areas connect young people to Native American wisdom about the natural world. Three books, *Keepers of the Earth*, *Keepers of the Animals*, and *Keepers of the Night*, published by Fulcrum Publishing in Golden, Colorado, offer selected Native American stories and field-tested, hands-on activities for the outdoors. Urban students have public zoos and museums of natural history as resources for the study of nature. I hope, or we should make it our hope, that students in the city can appreciate the night sky, and a visit to the planetarium becomes a promise some day to be in a part of our country where one can *see* the night sky.

Capturing the Surprises

Most of the fun of being outdoors is being in the right place at the right time. A frog croaks at the edge of a creek, leaps into the water, and then he is gone. A dragonfly hovers overhead, and then vanishes. Not too long ago, a red-tailed hawk swooped across the front of our car to snatch a rabbit on the grassy shoulder of the Meadowbrook Parkway as we whizzed by. I once saw a hornet fly into a spider web, and the tiny spider launched out to wrap up his generous catch, but when the spider got there, the hornet ate him! That's the way nature works. Now you see it, now you don't. Read Emily Dickinson's riddling description of a hummingbird in "A Route of Evanescence" for a sense of how ephemeral experience really is. Nature poems educate students to be receptive to the fleeting wonders of the natural world, and perhaps to the transience of all experience.

11

Scaffolding Poems

> Old houses were scaffolding once
> and workmen whistling.
>
> —T. E. Hulme

The ancient Greeks believed that poetry was not an art that could be taught, but an inspiration that came from a divine source. Poets were inspired and possessed by the gods; how else would you explain why no one could be taught to write like a poet, why so many listeners had the words of the poets on their tongues? Even today poets impress us with their almost magical gift of saying things in ways that surprise and delight us, inspire and galvanize us, or console and reassure us; it's as though they got it from heaven. How daunting it is then to ask a student (or a teacher) to write a poem. Not every student or teacher is a gifted poet or wordsmith. Not every novice writer feels the movement of inspiration. This chapter shows how to borrow from the inspiration, structure, and language of professional poets in order to create new poems by imitating an author and scaffolding the poem on the author's poem.

Writing a Dramatic Monologue

" 'That's my last duchess painted on the wall, looking as if she were alive,' " I announce, textbook open in my hand, as I point to the back wall. Seventeen of the thirty heads in class turn to see whatever it is I'm pointing to, thinking that perhaps they have missed something when they walked into the room at the start of the period. They see no painting and turn back to look at me.

I hold up my hand in gesture and shake my head, saying regretfully, " 'I call that piece a wonder now; Fra Pandolf's hands worked busily a day, and there she stands.'" With open hand held out, I gesture once again. One or two look back at the wall as if they missed something and the rest look at each other, a few rolling their eyes once more at what is happening in class. I begin laughing as some of them smile sheepishly, not knowing what's up, and I ask them why they turned and looked to the back of the room. They answer that my actions of pointing and my words made them think that something was present that they should take notice of. I tell them that I created that dramatic scene for them to understand how a poem can present a drama in which one person does all of the speaking.

Tone and Dramatic Monologue

Of course, I have memorized the opening lines to Robert Browning's dramatic monologue "My Last Duchess," and have spoken them as if I am that self-centered Duke who has put his wife away for not paying him the full homage he requires as a result of his heritage of a "nine-hundred-years-old name" and all of his wealth. I ask the students to open their books to the poem and I read those first four lines again before asking them to look at the fifth line: "Will't please you to sit and look at her?" I ask them what they understand from that last line and how it fits with the first four. We come soon enough to conclude that the speaker is talking to someone about a painting of his last Duchess who looks as if she is alive but may be dead. The speaker asks the other person if he'd like to sit and look at the painting. We agree that there are at least two people present, doing some action, and at least one of them speaks. I write on the board the words, "dramatic monologue" and explain that this is the name of the genre for such a poem and that they will eventually be trying to write such a poem themselves.

We spend about ten minutes reading the poem together and then I ask them what kind of person the speaker is, what is going on that causes this encounter, and what happened to the prior Duchess. I send them off to preassigned groups to discuss this poem for the next fifteen minutes while I circulate, listening to each group's suppositions, probing now and then, asking them to focus on a specific line that might redirect their discussion. We reconvene as a class and I ask the groups to report their findings. We learn of the Duke's arrogant opinion of himself, agree that he collects fine art, that he was upset with the Duchess for smiling as much at the little things in life as she did at his grand treasures, and that he somehow got rid of her. We also conclude that he is arranging for a new marriage and the person he is speaking to is there to arrange that agreement. We agree that the tone or attitude of the speaker's words are those of a self-centered, arrogant person of wealth and lineage. When I ask if the poet feels the same way, we conclude that Browning is holding up the Duke for the evil person he is through the subtle characterization in the form of this dramatic rendering.

Imitating What We Observe

My wife, an avid tennis fan, loves to watch tennis on TV. I myself have only recently returned to playing tennis, and didn't share her interest in watching the matches. However, attempting to improve my backhand shot, I realized that I needed some guidance with my footwork and swing preparation. While passing by the television one evening, I became interested in watching the swing and footwork of the players. As I stood and observed, I began to move my body around as if I were preparing to hit a backhand shot. I studied the player over and over and tried to imitate each move she made. My interest in watching increased because of my active participation in the game and a need to know. I found that when I played the next time, my stroke was a little smoother than before, though I might still use my forehand when an important shot comes my way. Nevertheless, my playing had improved and my appreciation for watching others play on television has become keener because of my playing.

The purpose for taking an entire period for this dramatic monologue lesson is to have students notice Browning's craft and how tone can create a character very different from that of the poet. All of this falls short, however, if the students don't get to try. It would be much like my trying to watch a tennis match to see how to hit a backhand shot without trying to hit one myself. My "players" need to write a dramatic monologue, working to create a character, unlike themselves, who comes alive by the tone of words spoken. I then show them my attempt at a dramatic monologue.

Failing Teacher Candidates
Look at this stuff. Garbage, all of it!
Nothing but junk from you these days!
You look at me with those big brown eyes,
about to brim over once again
but that's all foolishness and weakness on your part.
Stand up for once and face the facts.
I demand excellence of all of my interns
and your performance in class, your lesson plans,
your reflective journals—
all junk. I will not be embarrassed
to have one of my charges make me and the university
look incompetent, just because you can't do your part.
Oh, no! Don't protest! Put your hand down.
I've heard enough.
We can't let things like a mother in the hospital,
even if she does have cancer, stop us,
or a job that keeps you out till midnight
to pay for your broken down jalopy—
a throat infection that makes you tired—
No, those are excuses that take you down
from the very promising candidate you presented
in September, bouncing with enthusiasm,
answering my every email with wit and charm,
turning in papers that showed insight and skill.
My reputation is at stake, young lady, and
I suggest you shape up or face the—
Oh, please, use these to wipe away
your tears, and hush up your sobbing
or I'll end this meeting right now!
As I was saying, face the fact that
I will cut you loose from this program
just with the snap of my fingers
if you fail me ever again.
Now get your act together and
I'll see you next Thursday.
On your way out,
tell the waiting intern that
I'm ready for his silly excuses next.

Of course, none of my poem has the skill of Browning's couplets and the measured rhythm of his lines but I have taken a situation that I know something about and created a character with little empathy for the struggles of student teachers who are under his tutelage.

Trying Their Hand

I ask students to make a list in their writer's notebook of several situations in which there is a problem between two people over some object or some issue. Perhaps one of them is causing distress for the other in some way, such as a child, coming home late again, facing a parent, or a player coming out of a game and confronted by a coach. I suggest that they create one of these characters in a bad light and have either one of the speakers present the case in the form of a dramatic monologue. Or, if they want to take a bigger risk, try what Browning did and create two characters who are not at odds and yet have something in common about some object or situation. This could be a coach or advisor to a club or a boss, talking to the next captain or editor or employee about something the previous one created. They might imitate the tone that Browning used for the person in power.

We listen to some students share the items on their lists and then I ask them to try their hand at writing a dramatic monologue in keeping with the way Browning did it or the way I attempted it. I urge them to point to some object or person present and to say something about it to the person he or she is speaking to, the way I had my arrogant teacher point to the "stuff" from a student and the way Browning had his Duke point to the painting on the wall. The students spend the next ten minutes working on this and we listen to a few volunteers who read their work so far. At that point, my work on the dramatic monologue is all but over. I don't assign this form for all to do and to hand in. My goal has been to increase their appreciation for another kind of poetic form and to give them a chance to play around with it by scaffolding a form for them. The choice is then theirs to work on, to perfect it, to bring it to a polished state. I am available for a conference but I don't assign and collect such a work. Even in my former, more traditional approach to poetry, I would not have asked that the poem be handed in for a grade. I would have asked that their package of poems in imitation of ones we've studied be handed in as a unit for a grade, based on their effort to imitate these genres and styles. More recently, I've come to give students a choice of the kinds of things they would hand in as part of their quarterly writing portfolio. Some might have done a dramatic monologue while others might have imitated Emily Dickinson or Robert Frost.

Scaffolding Through Imitation

Jerry was reading a poem by Sharon Olds (1992) called "The Present Moment," which reminded him of a visit to see his father in a nursing home. He decided to follow Sharon Olds' structure and write about his own memories of his father. In her poem, Olds contrasts a picture of her father lying helplessly in a hospital bed with one of him as a younger man lying on a couch, taking a nap. She recalls many of the features of the more robust man who has since become a frail figure. She shows his not being able to sit up, only lying and staring at a wall. She says that she forgets how his reading glasses used to multiply the lights in the room when he put them on. She has used the word *now* at the start of the first two lines to show her father's frailty and then contrasts that with two actions of his alertness as he used to read the world around him. Here is Jerry's poem.

> **The Present Moment**
> Now that I see him in a wheelchair
> asleep in the day room,
> his chin pressed against his drool-covered bib,
> his hands clasped meekly between his thighs,
> I try to remember the one who would bound up
> the stairs of our Brooklyn apartment,
> two steps at a time,
> the wooden banisters shaking.
> Now that he refuses pureed food and grows thin,
> I try to remember the man with large arms
> who cooked in the kitchen
> and ate hearty meals:
> black marrow from beef bones,
> cow's tongue and pig knuckles,
> and meatloaf splashed with Louisiana Hot Sauce.
> It's as if I abandoned that ruddy man

91

who gave me my first sips of bitter beer
that tickled and burned a young boy's throat.
I have left behind that young man, my father,
that blue-eyed, blond-haired boy,
and my father long before I knew him,
a baby in Saratoga Springs
asleep in his mother's arms
the way he is sleeping now
with his chin tucked against his chest.
I sit beside him now the way I did as a boy
in the front seat of the car on the way
to clean St. Casimir's Church,
sitting silently as we did then,
when the early morning was
a blended holiness of silent city streets
and cloudless skies.

—*J. Matovcik*

Jerry followed Olds' structure of repeating the word *now* and contrasting it with *then* as he told of visiting his father who sat in a wheelchair in a nursing home shortly before he died. He borrows several of Olds' key words to say himself "I have left behind that young man, my father" and "I stay beside him." He uses the structure of the food that Olds' father ate to describe the food his own father ate and he finishes with a reference to being present in his frailty but being reminded of an earlier, healthier time. If you put the two poems together, one page on top of the other, and hold them up to the light, you would see that they are almost identical in the number of lines as well as in line length. It's as if a skeletal structure of five or six spaced-out phrases were tacked up on the wall for Jerry to use as he filled in his own story and details.

This scaffolding can be thought of as training wheels on a bicycle. Eventually, these aids come off as the rider learns balance and develops confidence. The riding done prior to the removal, however, is no less enjoyable or rewarding. Most riders are the ones to suggest removal because they restrict the speed and movement. Once they are removed, there is no looking back because the exhilaration of being on one's own is so great but the parent who stands there with the training wheels in his or her hands, watching the child move off, has recognized that the present moment has been made possible by the months of scaffolding.

Each year, I hand out a copy of Robert Frost's poem, "The Pasture," and write on the board this question: "What is present in this poem that would cause Frost to place it at the front of the volume of his collected works, separating it from all of the other poems, placing it even before the table of contents?" Then students follow along as I attempt to imitate Frost by reading with a New England twang the way I've heard him read his works on records and tapes. Sometimes I have students do a think along (see Chapter 14), but if it's early in the school year and I haven't introduced that strategy yet, we unpack this poem together. The poem consists of two stanzas, the first line of each announcing something the speaker is going to do, such as clearing the pasture spring and checking on the newly born calf. We then play a little game called "What Do We Know or Notice?" in which I ask students to list quickly as many things as they can about the poem, from the very obvious and seemingly simple to the more complex and interpretive. These could be as simple as seeing that both first lines contain the same first four words or that both are tasks the person seems to look forward to. I then go around the room and ask students what they noticed. Looking at all of their contributions, students soon see the poem as an invitation to a friend or family member to join the speaker as he does a simple but pleasurable farm task. I return to the initial question about Frost's purpose in placing the poem at the start of the collection. Eventually, we come to see that the poem is an invitation to the reader to come along on the poetic journey that collection will present.

On the copy of the poem that I had handed out earlier in the lesson is a series of words or syllables of words from the poem. Since "The Pasture" is written in iambic pentameter, each line contains an unaccented word or syllable, followed by an accented one. The poem begins with the words, "I'm going out to clear the pasture spring"; I have written to the right of the poem, "Go, out, clear, past, spring," representing the five accented syllables in the line. I show this to students and we beat out the five words to my cadence. Then they say it with me. Next I read the full line and we tap out the same five accented syllables. I have provided the same kinds of activity for the next two lines of the poem and we repeat this exercise. I show them that entire poem follows this pattern in its invitation. Then I ask them to think of a task or activity that is not at all unpleasant, even pleasurable, and have them invite a family member or friend to accompany them. Their challenge is to try to follow Frost's pattern.

Frost once said that writing poetry without rhyme or rhythm was like trying to play tennis without a net. In this activity, students see how easily Frost seems to have created his poem but how hard it actually is. Some struggle mightily while others get it soon enough. After about ten minutes, I tell them that I want them to complete this poem but in the process, they might want to change the rhyme scheme or eliminate it and just have a rhythm. What follows is the poem that Jerry wrote as his invitation.

The Beach Dunes

I'm going out to walk along the shore;
I'll stop to pick up beach plum in the sun
(And watch how fiddler crabs could sideways run)
I shan't be gone long—you come too.

I'm going out along the boggy creek,
Among the marsh grasses to catch a sight
Of a snowy egret's curved neck, so white.
I shan't be gone long—you come too.

There are scores of poems that teachers can use for this activity. We have used William Carlos Williams' "The Red Wheelbarrow" in a similar way with students eventually writing their own poem that begins with the words "so much depends/ upon" and following the same kind of structure that Williams used, once we have discussed it. An excellent book that provides great examples is Sharon Creech's novel in poetic form, *Love That Dog*, the story of a fifth-grade teacher who feeds her students good poems without overanalyzing them, and a student who writes a poem back to her each time imitating the poem she has given to them. Students might even try to using the scaffolds they found in some of the poems.

Alan, an eleventh grader, tried to imitate Robert Frost and Emily Dickinson, as a result of reading their poetry. Here is his Dickinson imitation.

Rocking placidly on Wraparound porches—
Watching nature at Work—
The breeze comes Rustling through—

94

Rustic North Country Road—
Carrying a scented—
Revolution—to Spring

Crocuses from forgotten bulbs—
Emerge from—our memories—
Forsythia hedges Spring Forth—
Prophetic yellow swords—
Stabbing the air—Splendidly—
Verdant Branches of Life—
Appear to grow—As do we All—
Yet mankind doesn't have—the annual—
Setback—Autumn

—*Alan Lemley*

When students get to play around, imitating other poets, dressing up in their stylistic robes, using the scaffolds of skilled writers, they amaze themselves and us, providing us "Splendidly—with Verdant Branches of Life."

12

Rollicking with Bruegel
Responding to Art

Jerry Matovcik

Art makes life, makes interest, makes importance.

—Henry James

A few years ago my wife and I visited MOMA (the Museum of Modern Art) in New York City with my nephew, Charles, a tall, energetic adolescent who loved rap music and wanted to be a DJ. When he saw some of the unusual art work at the museum, he laughed out loud. One might think he was being disrespectful if one thinks that museums should be as serious and somber as libraries. On the other hand, I found Charles' reaction refreshing not only because it was genuine but because Charles instinctively understood something of the humor, satire, and irony of modern art. Picasso's making a bull's head out of a common bicycle seat and handlebars is pretty funny and clever. So is Alberto Giocometti's thin, elongated bronze cat who appears to be roaming a back alley for a few fish bones. What would be your reaction to rows of sand lime bricks stacked neatly on a gallery floor as though left by some fastidious workman? Such minimalist sculptures play with our judgment and our preconceptions. Sometimes we assume that art is always serious. I think teachers should keep this playfulness in mind when we ask students to respond to art. The art belongs to our students as much as it does to teachers and critics. By encouraging students to write poems in response to art, we are encouraging students to trust what they observe and feel.

One poet who enjoyed the energy and playfulness of art was William Carlos Williams. I often introduce art poems with Williams' response to Pieter Bruegel's *The Peasant Dance*, a raucous scene of peasants at a religious feast, drinking, playing music, and dancing. Bruegel, a Flemish townsman, painted robust scenes of rustic life to point out the foibles of human nature that were more obvious in the behavior of peasants than in the proper manners of the upper class. Using an overhead color transparency, I invite students into the scene, saying, "Step inside the painting and walk around, and tell me what you see." For many works, it is best to divide the painting into sections so that the viewing isn't overwhelming. You can divide the work into foreground, middle ground, and background, or view the bottom third, middle third, and top third.

The Peasant Dance

In the foreground of *The Peasant Dance*, Bruegel paints children playing as miniature adults in adult clothing. In the middle ground, on the left, we see the peasants drinking tankards of beer, their ruddy cheeks and noses glowing. A couple stands at the trestle table kissing each other on the lips while a lusty piper puffs his cheeks to play a hearty reel on his bagpipe. On the right side, an older man pulls his wife onto the dance floor with such energy that they pull us into the picture as well. The warm earth tones of peasant clothing, landscape, and pageantry cheer our hearts. In the background, more couples join the exuberant dance; a jester entertains a band of onlookers. The hefty drinking and hearty dancing are perhaps some small respite from the toil and fatigue of a peasant's burdensome life. If students "step inside the painting" with their senses alert, they will hear the bagpipe's drone, smell the homemade brew (or the bad breath of the peasants), touch the weathered faces of these laborers, and feast on the festive colors.

To train students to be alert to detail, I ask them to play detective and list any artifacts in the painting that might have gone unnoticed on first view. For example, the purse and key that dangles from the belt of the woman racing onto the dance floor suggests that she has some wealth that she could lock away. The broken handle from a clay jug on the bottom right, as well as the large spoon tucked into the male dancer's cap are, perhaps, a visual shorthand for the gluttony and mild greed of the partygoers.

97

After we discuss the painting, I read "The Dance," a William Carlos Williams poem in response to the painting. In the poem, Williams deliberately runs one line over to the next to mimic the movement of the dancers at the feast as they go round and around. This enjambement (of lines running into each other) in the poem creates a whirling sensation, which, in conjunction with clattering consonance and internal rhymes, threatens to spin the dancers out of control and send the brew spilling from clay jugs. The poem is a good example of form following function, that is, the way a poem looks follows what it is supposed to do, but for our purposes, it is a better example of how a viewer, like William Carlos Williams, truly enjoys a work of art by capturing its mood.

This procedure—a close examination of a painting on an overhead projector and a study of how a professional poet responded to it—can be done on a number of works of art. There have been many poets who have written in response to art, and can be used as models for students. Here are some suggestions.

Painting/Artist	Poem/Author
Landscape with the Fall of Icarus, Pieter Bruegel	"Musee des Beaux Arts," W. H. Auden
Starry Night, Vincent Van Gogh	"The Starry Night," Anne Sexton
The Disasters of War, Francisco José de Goya	"In Goya's Greatest Scenes," Lawrence Ferlinghetti
The Third of May, 1808, Francisco José de Goya	"Goya's 'Third of May, 1808,'" David Gewanter
Dance (first version), Henri Matisse	"Matisse's Dance," Natalie Safir
Equestrienne, Marc Chagall	"Don't Let That Horse," Lawrence Ferlinghetti

Before starting a unit on poems in response to art, you might want to get students thinking about the larger concept of the role of art in culture. To spark some thinking along these lines, you might try some of the following statements about art by prominent artists and critics:

"Art remains the one way possible of speaking the truth." —Robert Browning

"Art has as much reason for being as the earth and the sun." —Ralph Waldo Emerson

"Art comes to you proposing frankly to give nothing but the highest quality to your moments." —Walter Pater

"The object of painting is not to reflect the visible but to make visible." —Paul Klee

"Art is accusation, expression, passion." —Günter Grass

"All serious art is a criticism of life . . . the construct of the artist is a counter-statement to the world. . . . It says that things might be (have been, shall be) otherwise." —George Steiner

"Art is meant to disturb." —Georges Braque

"Art is an epiphany in a coffee cup." —Elizabeth Murray

Another approach to teaching student response to art is to have the class look at a work of art, discuss it, and then respond to it in the form of freewriting. A good painting to use for this approach is Andrew Wyeth's *Christina's World*. This work has an air of mystery: is this stark landscape the only world Christina knows? And who is Christina, this woman whose face we cannot see? Such open-ended works of art are a source for rich response. Again, I invite the class to "take a walk" through the scene of the painting to see what we discover. There is Christina in the foreground lying in a field of dormant grass, leaning toward an old worn house in the distance. Christina looks pale and sickly; the wisps of her black hair echo the wisps of dry grass as well as the dark black crows that scurry from a deserted barn. Christina's pink dress looks as fragile (or as strong?) as a weather-beaten lobster shell tossed upon a New England shoreline. The purpose of this exercise is to notice the details we might have missed in a cursory view. Then I ask the students to freewrite their response to the painting for five minutes in their notebooks in the form of a poem. I ask students to imagine who Christina might be and what her story is. Students could write her story in the third person, or they might try writing in the first person so readers could get inside Christina's mind.

I encourage students to choose paintings that spark some kind of narrative response or emotional reaction. I steer students away from beautiful landscapes and floral paintings because, in the end, there is no story to be told and very little for an average writer to write about. I offered some paintings filled with dynamic action to a group of eleventh graders who needed extended time in English in preparation for a comprehensive state examination. One of my eleventh graders, Curtis, chose Winslow Homer's *The Lifeline*, a dramatic scene of a sea rescue in which a lifeguard is sent out to a foundering ship in a storm to save a young woman. Winslow Homer wrote about seeing such a rescue off the shores of New Jersey. When a ship is torn apart by a storm and sinking, the sailors initiate the rescue by throwing a rope overboard attached to a buoy. The crashing waves take the buoy to shore where it is attached to a block and tackle, and a lifeline is constructed.

I explained to Curtis that the painting, *The Lifeline*, became controversial because of the sensual figure of the woman who lies cradled in the strong arms of the lifeguard. The pose of the young woman and the fact that her dress exposes some of her leg offended many viewers in the nineteenth century who found the scene immodest. According to one story (which may not be true), Homer later painted in the red scarf over the lifeguard's face so the lifeguard would not be seen gazing at the young woman's face. In the poem that Curtis wrote in response to the painting, he captures some of the turbulent emotions that run through the lifeguard's psyche as he attempts the rescue, emotions that reflect the thrashing waves and tossing seas around him. When Curtis was looking for a word to describe how the young woman vanishes from the rescuer's arms, a friend of his in class, who was taking a woodworking class at the time, gave him the interesting word *feathering*. In woodworking, one feathers the edge of a piece of wooden molding with sandpaper, reducing the edge until it blends with the rest of the piece.

The Lifeline by Winslow Homer

I react subconsciously.
Each second an eternity.
Water glistens on her elegant, limp body.
I feel her strength within me.
The waves start to tangle with each other.
Fragrance from her shawl washes my salty face.
The lust for the shore becomes lost.
I want to hold her forever.

They take her away from me,
Breathing life into beauty.
Too shy to hold her hand, my own lifeline rips:

She becomes a myth, a mist in the wind,
Feathering off into a mirage,
Sought after like precious rubies in the night.

—*Curtis Caputo*

My ultimate goal for a unit on poems in response to art is to have the finished poem and the artwork matted and ready for framing. In this way the student writing becomes available for the appreciation of an audience; the writing does not wind up in some discarded class folder. When poem and picture are matted together, the art of writing shares an equal place with the art of painting and sculpture. The fairly recent availability of color photocopy machines has resulted in some impressive student projects. For about a dollar, students can make a color copy of any painting that looks as striking as the original print. The project also becomes an exercise in aesthetics as students select different colors and textures of designer paper, and different color fonts, for their poem. Finally they coordinate these choices with their painting. I approached the owner of a local art framing store to help with the matting, and she agreed to matte the poems and pictures for a nominal fee.

Daniela Gardner's matted poem, "Silent Love," is an example of this aesthetic process. Her poem is in response to Marc Chagall's painting, *Double Portrait with a Wine Glass*, one of the many paintings by Chagall celebrating his marriage to Bella Rosenfeld. Daniela printed her poem in green ink, which echoes the green water and Chagall's green vest in the painting. Her textured granite paper complements the textured sky in the left portion of the picture. The entire work was fixed in a golden matte to accent the sun and golden sky as well as the golden hues that resonate in the scene. Daniela's poem reminds us that although a painting is silent, it still speaks volumes about the love that it celebrates.

Silent Love
Angels bring them together.
A golden blessing sweeps the sky.
Day creeps to its peak—
A new ray of life.

Celebrating hearts toast strength and trust.
The brawn of love supported by faith.

Drinking red warmth,
He's wrapped in love.

Playful and charming,
Fruit of life, bold and content.
Colorful romance of earlier days
Covered in true shades of love.

Pure and untouched,
The white gown of virtue is torn by hues of found love.
Rooted, grounded and sturdy,
Quenched by a river,
Ambitious as the dream that sits on her shoulders.

Fitting each other,
Complete as one,
Sharing devotion,
A genuine love is painted in silence.

Producing poems in response to art is an opportunity for interdisciplinary study with an art teacher exploring various artists, movements, and styles. If one were to make a quick study of *Double Portrait with a Wine Glass,* one could trace the influences on Marc Chagall's style. The bright red jacket, green vest, and purple stockings are a tribute to the artist's Fauvist roots. The floating angel figure and balancing lovers standing over the city of Vitebsk are in the Surrealist mode, while the angular geometric shapes of the figures and planes of color recall the Cubist aim of representing objects from several points of view. Of course, one does not have to be an art expert to direct students in responding to art. In fact, overanalyzing a painting could result in an overly analytical poem that lacks spontaneity. Daniela was not educated in the influences on Chagall's art before she wrote her poem.

Another approach to a successful unit of art poems is to write a minigrant proposal. I wrote such a proposal for four hundred dollars in state funds through our local Mid-East Suffolk Teacher Center for an art response project entitled: "The Painted Word: From Art to Poetry." In the three-page application, I had to write a statement of purpose, list the project objectives, and describe my procedures and anticipated outcomes. I also had to describe my evaluation process and assessment criteria. Funding from the grant defrayed the costs of the matting and also went toward the purchase of designer paper, art books, and art CD-ROMs. If teachers do not have opportunities for grant money, the project could still be a success with modest resources. All one would need is a ream of cream-colored, granite-textured paper, a dollar from each student for a color photocopy, a paper cutter borrowed from central office, and some glue sticks. Students could print their poem on one sheet of designer paper and glue stick their illustration onto another, placing each sheet into a plastic jacket. I like to borrow as many oversized art books as I can from the local library (anthologies of masterpieces as well as books on particular artists). These books are the best sources to make copies of color prints. There are a number of excellent websites to find the perfect painting to respond to, although a copy of a print from the Internet is only as good as the quality of photo paper one uses and the quality of one's printer. I recommend the following sites:

www.artchive.com

www.artcyclopedia.com

www.bc.edu/bc_org/avp/cas/fnart/Artweb.html

http://sunsite.dk/cgfa/fineart.htm#indtop

You might start by examining the extensive lists of artists on www.artchive.com to suggest particular works for your students.

What follows are a few examples of the poems that came out of my mini-grant project with my eleventh-grade students. Athena's poem is actually a fine "reading" of Degas' painting and helps the viewer appreciate the artist's work even more. When I read Athena's poem, with its careful judgment and discerning eye, I am reminded of Iris Murdoch's observation about education: "The visual is an image of distance and non-possession. This idea of space and quietness, thinking, seeing, attending, keeping still, not seizing, is important in all education, and not only (where of course it is vital) in the appreciation of art" (1992, 462).

The Dance Foyer at the Opera by Degas

Graceful ballerinas at their first dress rehearsal
Wear new tutus which are unfamiliar
On their bodies—soft yet stiff while in motion,
Like a new born baby in the hands of a stranger.
Through the window the sun beams.

The light plays off their agile feet,
Casting a pink glow of pain and joy.

The dancer with the black sash
Performs by herself, solitary yet tranquil.
The others gaze in awe and admiration
Along with the violin player,
Who performs in unison,
His music glowing off the page as he plays.
The dance master looks on,
Stopping her by hammering his cane
Like a judge striking his gavel in court.

A lone chair sits in the middle of the room,
A red fan with a white sash resting upon it
With its shaky legs of wood.
Sorrowful drafts of fatigue waft through the doorway.
Years of practice have come to this one day,
The beauty of the dance has yet to begin.

—*Athena Lu*

Like many people, young and old, Evann was drawn to the disturbing images and anamorphous forms of Salvador Dali's surrealist paintings. While the painting is Dali's response to the Spanish Civil War, the imagery is universal and archetypal.

The Visage of War by Salvador Dali
Can you feel the pain of war?
We hear your screams bellow from barren, forgotten wastelands.
We see the horror of war in your eyes,
As the beasts, these signs of Satan, slither out of every pore.

Your last marks on this world are your bleached-white bones.
Your skin starts to leather and crack like the mud flats.

The war goes on:
    Spaniard killing Spaniard,
    Father killing son,
    Brother killing brother . . .

For what cause?

Are you nothing more than a pawn?
Your body fades as your existence has so long ago.
Another soul lost, another child killed, with years-deep dust
    it covers your remains.

You have become a FORGOTTEN, and PAST, visage of war.

                    —*Evann Devaux*

Don't be afraid to use art in the classroom. You do not have to be an aesthete or an expert in art history. You just have to enjoy what you are looking at, and show students how to enjoy the experience too, allowing the painting or sculpture to work its magic on you and feel confident in your response. Sister Wendy Beckett, an art historian well-known from her PBS television series, has shown us the way: instead of lecturing her audiences on color, line, texture, and shape; she speaks about the joy or sadness that an artist felt in his own life; she describes the range of emotions that the art evokes in herself; she makes connections between the work and her own life, rollicking in all the ways she can.

13

Finding Out When You Write Best

My son Brian sent me a copy of Billy Collins' anthology of contemporary poems for Father's Day, called *Poetry 180: A Turning Back to Poetry* (2003). Brian loved all of the work of Billy Collins but he thought, since I have always been involved with introducing high school students to poetry, that *Poetry 180* would fit my needs. He was right about that. Two weeks later, on a Sunday morning in late June when my wife was away for the weekend and the house was empty, I found myself getting up very early, perhaps before 5:00 A.M., going down to the kitchen with my copy of *Poetry 180* for a cup of coffee and some reading in perfect solitude. As I sat on a stool by the counter next to the windows that look out to the front lawn and street, reading and sipping coffee, some movement out on the street caught my attention and, in a matter of seconds, was gone. It was a teenaged boy on roller blades, delivering newspapers. I was struck by the uniqueness of it all and wrote the details on a large Post-It note, using the front and the back. I soon went up to my computer and typed the following poem.

> **On Reading Billy Collins' *Poetry 180* on a Sunday Morning**
> A strapping boy of about 17,
> in tank top and black pants,
> glides past my window at 7:05 on a Sunday morning
> as I sit perched on a little stepladder
> in my furniture-less kitchen, reading
> poems and
> wondering if I could ever
> write a poem like Billy Collins,
> Ted Kooser,
> and Jan Heller Levi, whose

poems I have just read aloud
to myself
in this empty house.

The boy is gone in a blink,
having roller bladed out of my life,
pushing an old red wheelbarrow with a balloon tire,
the barrow filled with plastic wrapped newspapers.

He zipped past my window view in three seconds,
too little time for me to get down from
this little stepladder and crane my head
for a longer look to double-check my eyes.

Perhaps he is the one who will deliver
my Sunday paper on his way back . . . but
not yet
so I am content
with my poetry and Billy Collins.

The point to all of this is that I know when I am able to write creatively, to compose a poem like this one. I need solitude, some poem(s) to get me thinking poetry, a blank table or counter, a pen and some paper or my writer's notebook. I can't work at a crowded desk or in a place with noise or distractions. I also have a very hard time composing first on the computer. I have come to know that over time. I also know that I write the best very early in the morning, though I am not by nature an early riser.

Most students don't know any of this about their optimum composing conditions because almost all of their writing is assigned for a particular date and time. On the very rare occasions when they are even asked or allowed to write a poem, they are given a time and perhaps even a topic. They don't get the opportunities I have of discovering an event and then writing about it, and they don't get the chance to rise early or work late because the assignment is set for a certain date. I discuss these writing conditions with my students and ask them to consider how they can coax out the poems that are in hiding for them.

One of the benefits of the workshop setting that Jerry and I have used for years is the lack of specific assignments and dates for any one assignment or task. When we give minilessons and then ask students to try a particular genre or technique right then, the students do so in their notebooks and then are usually free to develop it further, as I did by going to the computer and crafting the notes I had written. We believe in allowing ideas to gush forth onto the page, trusting them as being of worth. We add that the gush is not enough; the pouring forth of ideas and emotions needs to be shaped, using the tools and skills that are part of the teacher's repertoire of lessons and minilessons. However, we also need to have faith in our students that they will discover the times when they produce their best work and they will learn what inspires them to write in the first place. Most, upon reflection, will learn that they work best at night, sometimes even in the wee hours of the morning, and often as a result of listening to a song or looking at a CD album cover. This is no small thing for them to learn. Once they know, they can more easily re-create those conditions to continue producing effective writing.

14

Think Along
Unpacking the Poem

How many times have we heard students remark that they hate reading and analyzing poems because they can never figure out the symbols or see the meanings that their teachers find in a poem? Their complaints are not very different from those about their struggles with novels and plays that appear so easy for their teachers but so obscure for them. Some teachers just tell students the "real meaning" because it's easier than facing their puzzled, lost looks and stares. At the same time, in recent years, I've noticed a sharp decline in student reading. Whereas most strong students in years prior would do the assigned readings from novels and other texts, more and more now seem to find other ways to get around reading with summaries and other means. Weaker readers don't seem to give much of an effort at all. Because a greater number of students in the past still did their reading, many of them picked up the reading strategies that competent readers have largely taken for granted. In my case, because I had just assumed that readers read, I never considered the need to show students the sophisticated reading strategies to make meaning, never mind give them the guided practice that is necessary for increasingly difficult texts. These texts often deal with irony, satire, dense or complex sentence structure, and genres unfamiliar to students and are the very texts that students face in middle school and high school. Jeff Wilhelm, in many of his books including *Reading Is Seeing* (2004), has addressed the need for this kind of direct instruction. Kylene Beers in *When Kids Can't Read, What Teachers Can Do* (2003) presents some helpful approaches for improving the reading skills of all readers, not just the struggling ones.

Think Along

I've found success at developing student confidence with challenging texts by using a variation of Kylene Beers' Say Something strategy and her Think Aloud in what I call Think Along. I'll take a poem such as Mary Oliver's "The Journey" or Linda Pasten's "Possibilities," retype it, reduce the font size, and place it on the left side of the page, leaving blank three-quarters of the space to the right of the poem. Then I clump two to four lines together and create blank spaces below those lines before I do the same for the next group of lines. At the top of the page, I number the six or seven reading strategies that I will demonstrate and discuss with students. These include:

1. Restate
2. Paraphrase
3. Interpret a Question
4. Predict
5. Guess
6. Connect
7. Infer
8. Question

Below that and to the right of the first cluster of lines, in a space of about six inches wide and one inch high, I hand write an example of my own thinking along, using many of the eight strategies, numbering each move I've made.

In Linda Pasten's "Possibilities," the speaker begins by thinking about her having driven past a house they almost bought and, having heard music coming out from an open window, she considers how this family is different from her own. To the right of these five lines, I write:

> The speaker thinks back to earlier in the day when she drove past a house her family considered buying but did not. (*Restate*) I don't know if she was a kid then or a parent (*Question*) but they obviously never bought the house. (*Infer*) By not doing that, they did different things, (*Connect*) creating other "possibilities." (*Connect–Title*) The speaker says she heard music through the window of the house (*Paraphrase*) so she must have been driving very slowly. (*Infer/Guess*) She seems to be wondering about that other family (*Connect*) and, in turn, her own family, which may be very different. (*Guess/Predict*)

In those ninety words, I have demonstrated several reading moves and, on the paper, I numbered them to correspond with the aforementioned strategies. There are other possible responses and strategies that could be applied to these lines. The important thing is that readers slow down and use these strategies to open up more of the text to them.

Students Practice

I ask students to try to do the same with the next cluster of lines. I make the clusters simple enough so that the students can come up with their own discoveries in small chunks. If they had to do this initially with the entire poem, they might go off track. Limiting the number of lines for them to explore helps them to focus on each word or phrase, examining possible nuances of these words. I ask students to turn to a peer and compare their thinking and then we listen to several variations. Students must always tell which of the strategies they used for each portion of their insight. I've found it essential to have this identification occur to reinforce the necessity of using all the tools at a reader's disposal. We listen to several examples, noting slight variations in meaning; we withhold further judgment and try the next cluster of lines. By the second and third tries, even the slower students are using a variety of moves and are able to come up with a more complete interpretation.

After we have read the cluster out loud, I give students about four minutes to write out their think along. I've discovered that this approach to a new poem slows the process down. In addition, something happens when students take time to write out their thoughts. The very act of writing clarifies ideas in their minds far more than if we just read the cluster and then discussed it. After we do this with several poems, students are more easily able to simply say something as they read each cluster; they have begun to internalize inference-making strategies as they grow more competent.

Sometimes I use Philip Booth's "First Lesson," in which a parent speaks to a daughter while giving the child a swimming lesson, encouraging the child to relax with her head back in his hand, trusting the parent. The parent speaks about the future and the need to learn to trust in oneself. One student worked through her own understanding, faltering a little at first, thinking that the parent was putting the child to bed. In the next stanza, she didn't recognize the word *gull*.

In class, she said that she would have recognized the word *sea gull* but not *gull*. From a lifesaving course she had taken, she used her prior knowledge about swimming to understand that a dead-man's float, referred to in the poem, has to do with water. From there, she concluded that the daughter was being given a swimming lesson, though she never connected it with the title and the word *lesson*. This is a common omission by students who rarely see the title as supplying any meaning for the poem. This would be an excellent place to reinforce the value of good titles in the poems that students write. In the end, the student was able to make sense of a poem by using a think along to apply reading strategies in small chunks. (See also Figure 14–1 for an example of a think along exercise.)

Other approaches to improve the way that students approach difficult poems include ones articulated by Beers (2003) and Wilhelm (2004) such as frontloading, Say Something, Tea Party, and many other engaging activities. The more we help students work through challenging poems, showing them how to use the strategies that all good readers use without realizing it, the less likely they are to complain about harder poems and the more likely they will be to include some similar kinds of techniques in the poems they write.

THINK ALONG Use all of the space below with your observations, questions, and guesses about what is going on in this poem. Have at least three moves and then label each move with the first letter by circling the first letter.
Restate, Paraphrase, Interpret, Predict, Guess, Connect, Infer, Question

THE LONGER WAY

1

Brian Mahoney

I always take the longer way,
the ugly scenic route; a landscape
made for troubled travel.
I follow detours to delay,
treading where the pavement
does not even measure gravel.

THE SPEAKER IS A TRAVELER (INFER) BECAUSE HE TAKES A LONGER ROUTE EVERY TIME/ALWAYS (RESTATE) WHERE DOES HE GO? (QUESTION) IS IT THE SAME PLACE EACH TIME? (QUES) HOW CAN SOMETHING BE BOTH UGLY + SCENIC? HE SAYS THE ROADS WERE "MADE FOR TROUBLED TRAVEL." (RESTATE) WHY ASK FOR TROUBLE IN YOUR TRAVELS? (QUES) MAYBE TRAVEL CAN MEAN OTHER THINGS (PREDICT). HE ALSO SEEMS TO LIKE OR WANT TO TAKE DETOURS. (PARAPHRASE).

2
The driven traverse metered spans,
but short cuts tend to take their toll.
But voyagers are lost on roads;

3
Such interstates are careful plans
to sew together cities where
a journeyman implodes.

4
I am not where I should be
by this watch and intersection;
my natural course is cause to stray.

5
I can not grasp this small cartography,
tardy to the simple destinations.
I always take the longer way.

Literal Level: This poem tells about a
situation in which

Interpretative Level: This poem on
another, deeper, level deals with the
issues of/ suggests

Figure 14–1 Think Along for a Poem

15

Poetry Circles

Going to a Museum

Thirty tenth-grade students walk around the perimeter of a classroom, alone or in groups of twos and threes, stopping every ten feet to read, and perhaps talk briefly about, a poem taped to the wall. Then they move on to the next poem. I taped two poems on each of the classrooms walls, poems that I thought might appeal to students. I told students that we would be working in groups with a poem of their choice but I wanted them to look over the selections first. They walked about the room, examining poems the way people view works of art in a museum. When they found a poem they liked enough to study over the next four days, they asked me for a copy of that poem, and returned to their seat. I told them that there were only five copies of each poem. They had to decide whether they wanted to get their poem early, before the five copies might be gone, or continue strolling about the room, looking at other poems in hopes of finding one even more appealing. Within ten minutes, students made their selections and everyone was seated, ready to discuss a poem, and, by the fourth day, do a dramatic presentation of it to the rest of the class.

I selected the poems from poetry books I had on hand. Generally, they were interesting poems with some sort of story line that might appeal to tenth graders. Today, I might turn to a collection of poems that was edited by former poet laureate of the United States Billy Collins, in a book called *Poetry 180: A Turning Back to Poetry* (2003). Collins has not only collected 180 contemporary poems but sees this book as doing a "180" in the way poetry has been presented to high school students. He has said that "all too often, high school is the place where poetry goes to die" (xvii). So Collins has collected poems that high school students might appreciate. He also uses the number 180 because that represents the number of days that most states require for school to be in session. Collins proposes reading a poem a day, just for enjoyment, not for analysis.

In addition to this printed collection, these poems can be found on a website (www.loc.gov/poetry/180) that Collins has established, along with a description of each poet. If I were to have students select poems for the literature circles activity, I would have them go to this website as a starting point. I would ask them to nominate poems and then vote for the most popular ones, thereby creating the groups as I had done with the poems I taped to the classroom walls.

This lesson took place in late April, right after I had returned from a spring conference of the National Council of Teachers of English (NCTE) at which I learned about literature circles from my friend Pat Monahan, who had used literature circles with great success with the novels his senior classes had read. I wanted to try this in my classroom but I didn't want to devote all of the time that it would take with a novel, a play, or even a short story. I wanted something that students could read quickly and discuss right away, since I was more interested in students talking and working with each other than I was in their reading a particular genre. I decided to use poems because I could photocopy them easily on a single sheet of paper and still give students room on the paper to mark up the text and to write on the bottom of the paper. Since poems have at least some percentage of the story below the surface and students have to dig to make inferences, I thought the group discussions might be lively and open to multiple interpretations.

Discussion Roles

While I was at NCTE, I also purchased a copy of Harvey Daniels' book *Literature Circles: Voice and Choice in the Student-Centered Classroom* (1994), and had read most of it before introducing the idea of literature circles to my students. I showed them the six roles that Daniels articulated in his book, suggesting that they might imitate one or more of these approaches as they prepared for their group discussions. The roles were Discussion Director, Vocabulary Enricher, Literary Luminary, Connector, Investigator, and Illustrator. It's interesting to note that Daniels reduced the importance of these roles in his revised edition

(2002) as he realized that they were too forced and contrived. That is not to say that the roles didn't represent the different ways that readers respond to texts. They defined those approaches very well and actually gave students practice in different ways to respond to a text, but they were like exercises, drills, that were often overused by teachers who didn't know when to take these training wheels off. The first thing I did after arranging students in a circle, based on the poem they had chosen, was to give out a description of the roles. Each of these descriptions had a short example or a prompt. Since there were five students in each group, I eliminated two of the roles that didn't seem appropriate—the Vocabulary Enricher and the Investigator—and asked two people to prepare for the pivotal role of Discussion Director because I wanted two people to prepare, just in case one of them was absent the next day when the discussions would take place. We read through these descriptions and discussed how many of these responses were similar to what they had been saying to their peers and to me in literary letters about the books they had been reading.

I then asked them to work silently for the few minutes left in the period, reading their poem and filling out some of the responses or reactions fitting their role. I also asked them to complete their notes at home in preparation for group discussions the next day. I told them that following fifteen to twenty minutes of discussion the next day, they were as a group to plan a dramatic rendering of the poem to the whole class on the third and fourth days and we, as a class, would discuss different options for these dramatic presentations. My purpose for this unit was to give students opportunities to talk with each other about a poem and to work collaboratively to make the poem enjoyable for the rest of the class. I did not want this to be one more school writing assignment in which students would write a literary analysis of a poem and hand it in for the teacher to read. They had done enough of that during the year. I wanted them to participate in a more celebratory reading of poetry.

Group Discussions

Before the next class started, I had written some general topics or questions on the board. I explained that their individual reactions and responses would probably lead to several of the bigger questions or ideas that can be asked about most poems.

- What happened or what was the story in this poem?
- Who was the speaker in this poem? Who told the story? Was there an "I" who spoke to the reader or to someone present? Who was the speaker?
- Was there a listener or someone else present? What can you say about that person?
- How did the speaker tell the account? What was the tone of voice? What was the speaker's attitude toward the people or events being recounted?
- Were there any troubling words, lines, or sections of the poem that made understanding the poem difficult?
- What point or points do you think the poet wanted to make in this poem?

I asked students to wrestle with these issues after they completed their discussion, based on their own responses to their individual roles.

After about twenty minutes of discussion, during which time I circulated among the groups, noting how each one was handling the process, I flicked the lights a couple of times, calling everybody's attention to the front of the room where I had written on the board, "Ways to dramatize/act out/re-create a poem." I asked them how different groups might do this. We came up with the following ways.

- Just act out the poem with different students assuming different character roles, including some students simply being a tree or a car, not having a speaking part.
- Have one or more students read the poem aloud, pausing at dramatic moments as others acted out the main actions, perhaps even miming them.
- Re-creating the central incident or issue of the poem without using the words of the poem but making up a new text or paraphrasing the original.
- Having a choral reading of the poem so that certain lines might be repeated, read in various tones, perhaps using multiple voices, maybe even with accompanying music, and with one or more students acting out the actions.

We discussed having variations to these activities, even writing poems in response to their poem. The choice was up to them. They would have the rest of the period to discuss what they wanted to do and then they would have the next day of class time to rehearse their dramatization. The fourth day would be for the actual performances.

Rehearsals

On the third day, I spent time circulating from group to group, watching their progress, asking questions when necessary, making suggestions when appropriate. The plan was to have each group's performance be five to seven minutes in length, followed by a minute or two for questions or reactions.

Showtime

On the fourth day, each group was scheduled to render their poem. Spirits were high as some groups paraded in with costumes and props that they thought would enhance their performance. Not all of the performances were as polished as we would like but all group members got to participate fully through discussions and dramatization. Everybody left the room on that last day having enjoyed themselves as they spent time working with others and fully engaged in poetry. None of them saw it as a dull studying of poems.

Fast-forward about seven months. In my first year of retirement, a district asked me to help them to observe all of the secondary English teachers in their high schools and middle schools. In one middle school class that I was observing, the teacher was using literature circles for the first or second time and seventh-grade students were meeting to discuss the novel each group had read. Instead of just sitting by myself during the time of these group discussions, I always moved to a group, introduced myself, and listened for a while. Occasionally, I would ask a question to spur the discussion but also so I might make some suggestions with the teacher in the postobservation conference when we would discuss the lesson. I would always ask the students if they liked this approach to discussing the novels. I remember the enthusiasm they all had for this activity, but I particularly remember one boy saying, "Yeah, we get to say what we think, and we don't have to sit all period and listen to what the teacher thinks. We get to think for ourselves and to talk to each other about it." The others in the group couldn't help adding, almost as a chorus, "Yeah, that's it. That's why we like it."

That seventh grader's response represents the fundamental thinking of Harvey Daniels (1994) and his work with literature circles. He is interested in promoting student choice as well as student voice. He knows that when activities are structured to allow for this voice and choice, students are very willing and capable of discovering far more than they might under a structure in which the teacher is the one leading all of the discussion and providing the focus and direction. Patrick Dias (1987) discovered the same thing in his research at the University of Toronto when he arranged to have middle school students discuss poems based on articulated roles but largely left on their own. He found that students, through small-group discussion and then a plenary involving the whole class, demonstrated much more than their teachers could ever even dream of their doing.

Evaluation

Since my students had been operating in a writing–reading workshop all year and would soon be starting on their final portfolio, my use of literature circles on this occasion was solely to promote group talk since most work they did during the year was done on an individual basis—reading books of their own choosing, writing literary letters to me and to peers about these books, and writing "finished" pieces of prose and poetry on topics and genres mostly of their own choosing. Though they worked in groups during these few days, they still had their own work to do for the fourth quarter, in this case, reading and writing outside of class, things they ordinarily did during class. Since the students knew how they were going to be evaluated for the quarter based on their reading and writing, I didn't need to come up with ways to evaluate them for these four days. They were practicing reading, writing, listening, and talking for a variety of purposes, covering quite a few of the New York State learning standards. They didn't need to get a grade to perform well here. The nature of the activity prompted them to perform well.

16

Poems Speaking to Poems

A passionate young man stares into the eyes of his beloved and pleads with her to come away with him and be his love. He promises her that he will show her all the pleasures of the world and they will enjoy lolling by rivers and streams in the beautiful summer air. We listen in on this plea and think that maybe, yes, he does have a good idea and that we should all just seize the moment and go for our dreams.

But wait! We listen to another voice, this time the girl whom the passionate youth had been addressing. Yet she is not gazing at him fondly and in an enraptured state, saying she will run off with him. Instead, she suggests that he isn't being realistic at all and asks what will they do when summer turns to winter and they have no place to go. She chastises him for his foolish idealism and says she will not run away with him and be his love.

This sounds as if it is a dialogue between two people in the same place and at the same time. But, in fact, it is the presentation of two views in two entirely separate poems, written by two different poets and written some years apart, both in the Elizabethan era. The first, by Christopher Marlowe, is called "The Passionate Shepherd to His Love," and the second, by Sir Walter Raleigh, is called "The Nymph's Reply to the Shepherd." Even the titles suggest a relationship. We could say that these two poems are talking to each other, poems speaking to poems, or *companion poems*, works that acknowledge an earlier work and advance the topic or provide a retort to the speaker of the first poem.

In a related vein, an eleventh grader was reading *Catcher in the Rye* (Salinger 1953) and decided to write a poem of response to something that Holden Caulfield said. When Holden visits a bar called Ernie's, he always sees a piano player whom he considers to be showing off by "putting all these dumb, show-offy ripples in the high notes and a lot of other very tricky stuff that gave me a pain in the ass" (84). Holden concludes by saying, "If I were a piano player, I'd play it in the goddam closet" (84). Jody wrote a poem using Holden's last line, not arguing against Holden but showing his agreement by telling how he also would "play it in the goddam closet." A poem responds to a text.

If I Were a Piano Player,
I'd Play It in the Goddam Closet
I wish I had some identity skill
So I could be linked through the soul
To some act.
And it would always make me happy
Even when I am blue. . . .
And white—
Like I'd seen a ghost.
I'd look at the ghost
And play the piano in the goddam closet.
And it feels good.
Like it wasn't just me playing
All alone in the goddam closet,
But it would be as if that goddam ghost
Had followed me in
And we were playing an angel-like duet.
Harmony of souls;
Like I was a spirit too.
Not just a sorry young man
With no skills.
If I were a piano player,
I'd play it in the goddam closet
Just me alone with something that could
Finally make me happy.

—*Jody Shenn*

A few years later, Kerri wrote this reflection in her portfolio and placed it next to her poem.

Reflection
Upon entering my English classroom one afternoon, I was not surprised to see yet another poem up on the overhead. Mr. Mahoney had been

showing us his favorite poems for the last couple of days, but none of them had been able to reach my soul as strongly as Jody's.

I, too, often wonder what type of a piano player I am since the only people that comment on my playing are my immediate family, and they love everything. Yet, at times I also wonder if I consider myself a true piano player. After all, I do not practice hours upon hours. However, if I don't play for a period of time, I begin to miss the music. I have become attached to the sounds that emerge from the touch of my fingertips. And so, I suppose I could call myself a piano player.

After reading Jody's poem, I felt somewhat compelled to write my own version. The phrases were already forming in my mind as I read through his poem again. Why? I don't know if I'll ever figure that out.

If I Were Honestly a Piano Player . . .
(a response to Jody Shenn's original poem)
I wish I possessed just one skill,
One with the ability to identify me,
Setting me apart from the rest of the world
Of black
And white keys,
Bobbing up and down
In this universe of confusion.

And I wish this skill could be shown
In goddam wide open air
And not in Holden's closet of talent.
I'd feel good
If I had this identity skill,
But I would never realize any skill
Until it was brought into the open air
By a fellow player.

Then, I could live on
With something finally making me happy.
For I would play alone
And there would be no ghost of white
Tapping down on my territory.
I would play the same angel-like melody.
Instead, mine would contain more fury.
More hidden goddam closet skill.

—*Kerri Bianchet*

Adrienne was another student who used one poem as a basis for the second poem but in her case, she was the author of both poems.

Shellfisher
Waking before the sun,
I climb wearily out of my warm cocoon.
As if still asleep,
I prepare for my day's work.
Before long, I am there,
the Sound breathing before me,
a living spirit swathed in a blanket of mud.
The caresses of the sun warm my mind,
but the reality of April weather
numbs my fingers.
I allow myself a brief moment before I
plunge deep into my work.
This is my life now,
searching with skilled fingers for those
encasings of life, smooth or barnacled,
holding with fleshy folds of life.
I begin each morning,
concentrating solely on finding more.
But before long, I become
a modern muse, dreaming up
poetry in the mud.

Then she wrote "Apology to the Shellfisher," followed by her reflection.

Apology to the Shellfisher
My sincerest apologies to the shellfisher,
Whose life I romanticized in my poem entitled
"Shellfisher," in which I created a dream world
from not
my witnessing of your life, but from the
idealistic world in my head to, where digging up
"encasings of life" is the job of the poet musing in the mud.
I know of the harsh conditions which you must face,
The biting, premature winter winds and the
Leftover frosts in the spring;
I know of the cold, reeking mud (although

I have grown to love this smell) through which you must
Pull your heavy rubber boots;
I know that you must come home every day,
With an aching back, sore from bending over
To search for round little objects;
I know your life is one of physical hardship,
And you cannot waste time loafing around dreaming of
A world of poetical injustice. Forgive me for this
Fantasy: I have seen you often, yet never heard your story,
So I took the liberty of creating
A modest, yet enviable life for you.

—*Adrienne Lu*

"Shellfisher" is a poem I wrote for the Walt Whitman Poetry Contest. I was inspired by the shellfishers I see nearly everyday in Mount Sinai Harbor (close to where I live). After I won a prize for the poem, though, I felt very guilty because I know shellfishing cannot be easy. As a result, I wrote an apology to the shellfisher who might have been insulted by my romantic vision of his/her life. I think "Apology to the Shellfisher" actually ended up being a better poem than the original!

Getting Started

Select a poem that is easy enough for your students to understand and yet has enough complexity so that students can see options in developing their poem. One such poem might be "Mother to Son" by Langston Hughes because students could choose to have the son respond or they could present the father's words, talking to the same son. In the first case, the son might be very sympathetic to the mother's ideas or his words might be the ones that spurred the mother to speak in the first place. The son might have been complaining about how his life, with all of the good things his mother has sacrificed for him, has been unfair to him. If students chose the father's response, they could let the father deliver the same message but with different examples or they could present an apology for not providing as much for the son as the father wished he could.

With all of these possibilities, I would select one and show students how I begin. Using the overhead projector and a transparency, I would start to write about a boy who is discouraged with his lack of playing time on his baseball team and wants to quit.

> Life's not fair, Ma, it really isn't.

Then I ask students what he might say next and some say he might come right out and say he never plays, or that he's sat on the bench again or that the coach is not fair. I write those on the side in note form and then I write:

> You do everything people say
> and they still don't give you a chance to play.

During this writing, I have written words and then changed them for a better word, showing students that I don't always come up with the best words immediately. For example, I first wrote, "I do everything the coach says" but I changed the "I" to "You" because most people generalize before they are specific. I then changed "coach" to "they" for the same reason and I wrote "says" after originally writing "asks." To create a little more of a challenge, I point out that the mother compares her rough life to a staircase that is filled with obstacles, the opposite of a fancy crystal staircase. I ask students for some things the son might use to compare his tough problems and they suggest an unfair boss, a cheating bank, and a scam artist who takes money but doesn't give anything back. I ask students what might come next, take down some of their ideas, and write two more lines. I write:

> Life is a scam where they take your life savings
> and give you nothing back.
> They take all your sweat and hustle in practice
> and then tell you to take a seat on the bench.

At this point, I turn it over to the students to write four or five lines and then we listen to some of the variations. Since the Hughes poem has twenty lines, I urge them to write a similar number of lines but I also suggest that they might want to change the comparison or any of the lines so far, even starting from scratch with the boy or with any of the other options mentioned earlier. I have used what Nancie Atwell in a speech in San Diego (1995) has called "the handover," giving students the opportunity to work on their own and create a companion poem, a poem speaking to another poem.

After students do this activity a time or two, they will be ready to select their own poems for companion pieces. Even as I page through *Poetry 180*, edited by Billy Collins (2003), looking at titles, I am thinking of opposites or some variation. I see Gary Soto's lament at nothing to do at age seventeen in "Saturday at the Canal" and I think "wonderful times at the canal or creek or stream" or I think along with Gary but change the scene to Saturday at the local park, looking to "break out." As I look at Li-Young Lee's musings about a father–son relationship in "Words for Worry," I change his first line in which he says that a word for father is worry to "Another word for mother is suffer" or "Another word for teacher is care." All kinds of possibilities exist when students have options to try out and try on poems to see how they fit and then how they present options for poems of their own. The first poem can be used as a scaffold for the second one with the student using similar phrases and structures or it can be the basis for a student writing an opposite view or a response to the speaker in the first poem. In any case, the student begins to reconstruct is own world in terms of the view offered in the first poem and allows for walking around in the role, examining more possibilities than Gary Soto saw on that Saturday afternoon at the canal.

17

Poems About Writing
and Creating

I've long been interested in having students think about the composing process as that of an artist. I wanted them to see themselves as per-
sons who were capable in their present lives of making art out of the
arrangement of the words they had within them. To do this, I showed
them pieces in which writers appeared almost to be looking in a mir-
ror and seeing themselves doing the work of writing, creating, and
composing. That's similar to what Adrienne Lu had done with her
poem "The Shellfisher" (Chapter 16), in which she saw the composing process through the eyes of the shellfisher who was deep in thought,
making poetry in the mud as he worked. Other students have examined
the pain and pleasure of their own artistic endeavors. For example, Erin,
a ninth grader, considers the act of drawing her self-portrait—with
charcoal and in words.

A Portrait of an Artist as a Young Woman
She deftly sharpens her charcoal pencil,
and begins drawing herself drooling . . . err . . .
     1
dribbling
    toward the basket,
    the ball bouncing
off her foot and rolling down the court.
     2
gagging, she swallows the peas and
scowls at the mound of filthy dishes as she
plunges into the depths of

Palmolive . . .
    Palm . . .
        Pal . . .
            3
-Pal!
Kim, her friend of ten years (we counted).
        4
elle aime dormir, parce qu'elle est
            toujours fatiguee.
Translation: she likes to sleep, because
        She is always tired,
            which is why she is never on time.
                5
give her chocolate hazelnut truffles, and
she'll love you . . . and hate you.
                6
Music of all kinds wanders out of her speakers:
        James Taylor, Steve Miller, Jimmy Buffet,
        R. E. M., INXS, Billy Joel, Beethoven
        . . . Need I say more?
                7
A fault? <u>She's constantly underlining words.</u>
                8
Golden Brown, uh-
        BURNT marshmallows are
        among her greatest specialties.
                9
People call her crazy
        when she mentions wanting to try:
                sky diving
                bunji jumping
                hang gliding
<u>**AND**</u>
snow boarding
                but, hey,
        What the heck. You only live once.
                10
Her ambitions include: getting accepted to the

Chicago Art Institute (with a scholarship?)
and making **OODLES** of money someday.
>>11
Her dad, who thinks she's absent-minded, says,
>"She's always out to lunch."
>>12
This may be true, but her friends say,
>"She's very charming and creative."
Finished with her portrait,
>she lays down her pencil
>and sprays on the fixative
>>(so it won't smudge)
>>>—but don't forget, the signature . . .

>>>>>—*Erin Donnelly*

Jeff presents in his poem the struggles of writing and the need to take
risks as he works with an extended metaphor as well as the use of tran-
sitional words in each stanza.

Blowing in the Wind
The chimes of inspiration
Sway in the breeze of our thoughts.
As we ponder our ideas,
The winds of rejection roar in.

We try to deny them,
And go on with our creating.
But often the gusts overpower us
And we toss our ideas to the sky.

Yet there are some
Who are strong enough
To weather the criticisms
And float where they please.

These are the ones
Who survive it all
And wind up
In the heavens of print.

>>>>—*Jeff Heckelman*

How to Get Them Thinking

In a minilesson, I show my students one or two of these poems and ask them to consider how the poems might appear to an observer as they go about composing. At the same time, I ask them to think metaphorically (see Chapters 8 and 9 about extended metaphors) and compare their writing to some other creative arts, such as playing a musical instrument, sculpting, drawing, or dancing. I write on the board, "Writing a good poem (or story) is like playing a beautiful song on my guitar or violin or singing in the right key." I ask the students if anyone can describe what it's like when you are playing in the zone. They usually say that it is like floating and you lose all sense of time. Nothing else seems to matter. I then ask them to record in their writer's notebooks what it is like for each of them when they are in that zone in some creative act that they are good at. I urge them to think of the arts, but I tell them that it could as well be a sport. I ask them to describe specific actions that they take, such as moving their fingers along the keyboard or on the guitar strings, or feeling the seams and the tiny raised grains on the leather basketball as it sits cradled in their shooting hand. I ask them to concentrate on getting these details and then to write small. After about six to seven minutes, I ask them to stop and to turn to each other for a quick conference as they read some of their detailed descriptions to each other. I ask for volunteers to read their examples and I write some of the images on the board. Crystallizing some of these clear word choices is not only effective teaching but also another form of publishing for students, validating even a phrase or two in front of the whole class.

My Own Model

I read my own poem about my love of shooting a basketball but in it I have chosen to have the voice of a student describe what he thinks is the difference between making a beautiful jump shot and writing a poem.

> **Nothing but Net**
> My English teacher, Man,
> he don't know nothin'!
> All I want to think about is
> standin' 15 feet away and
> popping jump shots and

hearing the net snap
with each clear shot.
But this English teacher,
he wants you to write
deep stuff. "Write from
down here," he says and he slaps
his fat stomach. "Write from your gut!
with passion!"
That guy wouldn't know what passion is
with all of his poetry stuff.
I'd like to see him take three dribbles,
heading for the top of the key,
plant his right foot,
square up, look at the basket,
and then go straight up, letting
the leather ball, with its little ripples,
slide off his finger tips,
land on the same spot he left,
hit the floor, and go for the rebound.
Man, he just says to write about
what's real to you, and tell it true.
That guy don't know nothin' real.
So I'll just concentrate on my game
and let him talk away about his.

Sometimes the writer uses words to create art in another medium as Meghan does in the following poem about playing the piano, creating inner melodies that flow out in a way that words sometimes take wing.

Inner Melodies
These delicate, white, porcelain keys
beneath my rough, time-worn hands
are so easily pressed.
They seem to surround and envelop
my fingers,
allowing me to make the
most beautiful music.
Though the notes are
located before me
on the pages of this book,

the real notes are made and flow out
from within my heart.
I could not
play this piano
unless I had deep compassion
for making music.
Your soul must go into playing
every time you touch a single key.
Without emotion and truth,
the music is silent
to the ones listening.

—Meghan McGurk

Dan addressed his composing process by focus on the writing instrument that he referred to as his stylus. In his reflection, he wrote:

In this poem, I am showing the link between the life of a pen and how it is similar to the life of a person. People, like writing utensils, are tools that are used to create new ideas that will be recorded and kept in the memory banks of history. There are comparisons between the shape of the pen and a person's body: the blood with the ink, the motions that a pen is dragged through with the routine of millions of workers in society.

One day in English class, I was staring at the pen and paper, not knowing what to write, when I found the pen seemed to be staring me in the face. This work is another example of the different ways inspirations are formed for writing. When reading books of poetry, I've noticed that many celebrated works are comparisons of people to something else, be it an object, an animal, or even a piece of imagination. Perhaps my poem could be successful as well.

Stylus
I stand perfectly straight and
stare as the life flows
from inside me.
I just watch, because to try
to stop it is useless.
I am dying. Not now, but nevertheless, I am dying.

My blood, my ink, rolls down in perfect
lines and curves,

while my head twists and turns.

One can see just by the lines,
that I am fading.
Each day commences a new line.

And so am I. Gripped by humanity,
a tool to show that there
is strength, knowledge, and the will
to live.

—*Dan Ackerman*

Maura marvels at the mystery of the artist and celebrates the act of creating. When students walk in the shoes of the artist, they come to appreciate the effort so much more and bring that understanding to their own work.

The Artist

I marvel at what you see and find.
What appears gray and dull,
You see as mystical and magical.
And I benefit from your gift.

The words you put together
In rhythmic fashion
Send your song through my soul.
And I benefit from your gift.

The image you captured
Through your lens
Impacts and is etched in my mind.
And I benefit from your gift.

In your work,
I glimpse at your vision.
I can see it through your eyes, if only for a moment.
And I benefit from your gift.

—*Maura Brennan*

Mary compares her childhood love of creating words and images in the sand with her passion to record the memories of her soul by using a pen.

Poetry in the Sand
I celebrate through my mind and soul
the years of innocence
as a child of summer.
I absorbed the sand, becoming part of it as I dreamed.
I could feel the endless tablet in front of me,
Inviting me to create.

My finger was my tool flowing across the sand,
as smooth as a pen on paper.
From sunrise until the sun set everyday,
I created.
When I was writing, I was the sun,
A bright exterior,
warm inside and out.

The days quickly grew older, bringing me along.
My creations were consumed by the water
as the tides rose and fell to the likings of the moon.
Year after year, my tablet grew smaller
while the wind and rain banished pieces,
making them disappear into the vast ocean.

My pen is now the tool with which
I engrave memories into my soul
that are unlike the marking in the sand by a small child—
Vulnerable.

Paper has now become my tablet,
more confined, yet sophisticated.
I write now through my heart
as my mind once celebrated my years of innocence
as a child.

—Mary Zoccoli

Meghan writes about the pain that comes from taking risks in writing from her inner self and exposing who she is, and then being proud of the effort and the results.

Exposing the Core of Your Soul
My hands, cramped and sore,
Throb from pouring my heart out

Onto these lines.
The callused bump on my middle finger
Grows larger and harder
With each thought I spew out.

From these hands,
Life is brought to the page.
My life.
My story.
In everything I write.
There is a part of me.

I write till I ache,
And then I write more.
When the ideas disappear,
I rest my head,
Waiting for my mind to clear.
Once again, I pick up my pen
And write until I'm empty.

I will not edit—
A promise I've made.
How can you change
What you're feeling right then?
If you foster your thoughts,
They are no longer truly yours.
Feelings are not meant to be corrected.
A true writer realizes this
And understands.
There is nothing more perfect than the truth:
Getting to the core of your soul
And exposing it;
Subjecting yourself to an invasion
And being proud of what you've done.

—*Meghan Delaney*

Erin, a student in my ninth-grade class, loved the art of Claude Monet and upon receiving a gift of one of his paintings, wrote the following poem.

My New Monet
Claude Monet
and his artistic brush
create creamy, blending colors,
which bring me to a hush.

My eyes dance
over the grayish-blues.
Oh! How my mind loves
The contrast of his blending hues.

"Femme Dans Les Fleurs"
Is French for "Ladies with the Flowers."
A simple name, but not as simple,
as the painting's emotion-filled powers.

—*Erin Powers*

When we give students the opportunity to examine their passions and to record the things they love about an activity and then we show them how to put those observations into a form that is creative in a different way, we extend their range and allow them to see how all the arts, and even sports or other activities that they engage in, can be acts of creation for them. In doing so, this re-creation helps them to re-create themselves.

18

Autobiographical Poems

Getting the Inside Story

We have a great desire in this country to learn about the personal and private lives of glamorous people and popular stars. Even in stories of scandal, we have a fascination with the lurid details of the individual. When a famous person dies, newspapers fill pages and pages recounting the person's accomplishments and TV specials do much the same. We seem to like biographies when we know the person. When I am enjoying a book, I will often turn to the back cover to find information about the author and perhaps even a picture. When my students create their final portfolios at the end of the year, they must write reflections on five of the pieces they've included. These explanations provide information on how and why the piece was written as well as some of the techniques the writer used. When teachers look at the portfolios that we bring to workshops, they become fascinated with this biographical background information, even finding some reflections more interesting than the pieces themselves.

With the idea of biography in mind, I ask my students to provide a picture and a brief biography of themselves for the readers of their portfolios. Some write prose sketches but many write autobiographical poems based on a model poem by Lawrence Ferlinghetti called "Autobiography." The poet starts by describing where he currently resides and how, in general terms, his life is going or has gone. Ferlinghetti uses the words of these first few lines to close the poem, after he has listed the big events of his life: "I am leading a quiet life at Mike's place every day." I ask our students to use this same structure to recount the important moves of their lives.

Providing Models

In addition to showing them Ferlinghetti's poem, I show them another poem called "Autobiography" (in Mahoney 2002, 41–42) by a friend and fellow English teacher, Rich Weismann, who provided us with the materials that he got from another good friend, Bill Picchioni. Rich reflects on his teaching career in his opening lines.

> I have heard the clang of 10,000 lockers
> and stalked the tiled hallways past
> miles and miles of kaleidoscope classrooms.

And the poem ends . . .

> I tip-toed past Watergate, the Ayatollah,
> gas lines, leisure suits, Reaganomics,
> bull markets, baby boomers, and gray hair.
> But the clang of lockers
> and the drone of voices
> still call cadence for my march.

Mary, an eleventh grader, understood the idea of beginning and ending with similar words but she chose to use a structure from *The Prophet* for the scaffold of her poem.

> **What a Trip . . .**
> I too have learned how to be silent
> from those who are never quiet,
> Love from the unloving,
> and care from the uncaring.
> I will be indebted
> to these teachers.
> I have heard the voices of the angels;
> the laughter of a child,
> and the whispers of 600 rumors.
> I have smelled the sweat of 10,000 soccer players;
> the cookies of my grandmother,
> and the socks of a room full of friends.
> I have reached for the level of best;
> the hearts of my friends and family
> in hopes of making them stay.

I have seen loved ones leave me
never looking back,
and concerts.
I have felt the pain of loss;
the joy of victory
and the disappointment of defeat.
I once fell off a hamper
onto the floor
and in love.
I broke my arm;
my ankle
and a promise to a dear friend.
I have eaten pizza;
French fries
and spaghetti
all in one sitting.
I have grown upward;
inward
and outward
during the awkward years of my life.
I have achieved some great tasks;
goals once set
and hopes once dreamed
all in one lifetime.
I too have learned to be silent
from those who are never quiet,
Love from the unloving,
Care from the uncaring.
I will forever be indebted
to these teachers.

     —Mary Zoccoli

Marissa, a tenth grader, decided in her poem to have a variation between her beginning and ending lines in "The Scent of a Woman."

I lived a quiet life
settled in a house in Coram.
I used to play Barbie with my neighbors
and rode our bikes 'round the block.

. . .

I live a quiet life
settled in a house in Miller Place,
striving to be excellent, working to be happy,
but never forgetting the meaning of friends.

—*Marissa Lauryn Hahn*

I have used these autobiographical poems for a specific purpose in students' portfolios and have therefore introduced them late in the school year. Other teachers have used them at various times during the year with equally powerful results. Students seem to enjoy putting the highlights of their life into a list like this and enclosing it in the structure of repetition.

19

Evaluation

If you want to know what students can do,
you have to start by asking them to tell you.

—Donald Graves

"But how do you put a grade on such beautiful poems?" teachers ask me at workshops. They want to understand how I can put a number on a subjective work. I find it hard to answer briefly because of the unusual way I arrive at grades for everything that students do, including the final grades for the marking period. This evaluation process is fully detailed in *Power and Portfolios* (Mahoney 2002) but the short version is this: I never put a grade on any piece of writing that students do, nor do I give any tests throughout the year. This leads to their inevitable question of how I arrive at a grade for the quarter. I answer by showing how most people, including teachers, are not evaluated for their jobs on a daily basis and yet they manage to come to work every day and work diligently at whatever they do. Frequent evaluation has little bearing on their effort nor does reward or punishment. I believe students are no different in their approach to their work, though it may take time on their part to accept that idea, primarily because of the school culture they have grown up in that gives points for every act and everything results in a grade or some kind of reward. I believe that students will work diligently in school if they see how they will be evaluated and that the evaluation is fair and is meaningful to them. Part of this acceptance depends on their knowing beforehand the process for grading. If they understand this process, even though it may occur in chunks or over longer periods of time, they are quite capable of performing well under that structure. Anyone who thinks that high school students can't do this should observe a day at a fast food place where young people often run the operation from opening to closing, performing all of the responsible tasks in between.

Giving the Power

We all can be conditioned by rewards and punishments and do only as much as we want to get the rewards or avoid the punishments. We also see that when the punishments and rewards no longer apply, we tend not to do those activities that were spurred by the rewards or punishments. If we want students to see the inherent value of the work we do in class, we need to remove as many of those external rewards and punishments as we can and while participating in the final evaluations that school requires of us. As Victor Jaccarino (1996) said to me at NCTE in Chicago, "The secret is to withhold the grade for as long as possible." I've found that if I give students power and a say in how they are going to show what they had learned each marking period, they do not worry about grades and yet seem to work infinitely harder than they did under a "grade for everything" system.

My approach to grading in general was to ask students to produce about six or seven finished, polished pieces of writing a quarter, including essays, personal narratives, poems, dialogues, and many other types of writing. They would hand in this work at the end of the quarter in a portfolio, writing brief reflections about each piece. They would also annotate their writing, selecting about twelve skills, from a list of forty, that they wanted to show mastery of in the pieces and would write a sentence or two saying why or how the skill identified was working in each piece. For example, a student might highlight a simile or a metaphor and explain in the margin why the trait was effective in the piece of writing. Another example might cite the use of parallel structure and tell how it was used for effect. If students get to demonstrate what they've learned in the quarter and show how they used it in their writing, they don't have to worry about tricky quizzes and tests.

How can effective evaluation work in a more traditional classroom where grades in poetry are assigned for work as the units are completed? A teacher could grade in chunks, that is, in a block of poems rather than each and every poem that is written. This would avoid placing a grade on something a student wrote with a great deal of feeling or took a risk in trying something new. Instead, such a poem would be part of a package of poems demonstrating a particular theme or approach. At the same time, it is not necessary that a student submit a poem for everything studied or written in the quarter. I ask students to write lots of poetry in their writer's notebooks during the minilessons. Since such writing requires trying new things, they are free to experiment and to see what works for them. During any one marking period, they may see as many as fifteen to twenty different approaches or techniques. They couldn't possibly bring all of these pieces or types to completion so they have a choice of what they develop during the quarter. (It is not unusual for a student to return to the work of a previous marking period and to select something to bring to completion in the next market period.)

An example of students choosing different kinds of poems to bring to completion might look like this: in the third marking period let's say that students learned, among other things, three approaches to poetry. One approach was about poems written in response to other poems (see Chapter 16, Poems Speaking to Poems). A second was about poems written about the act of creating as in music, art, dance, and so on (see Chapter 17, Poems About Writing and Creating). The third type they learned was in preparation for their autobiographical sketch at the end of their portfolio (see Chapter 18, Autobiographical Poems). The teacher could ask for one poem from each of these types, to be submitted in a package, ranked and rated by the student for value or importance to the student. Or the teacher could ask for two or three poems of any type from the three units and each student would be free to experiment with two different versions of the autobiographical poem and one of the other two types. Another student might have wanted to do a collage of poems in response to the arts and decided not to complete any of the other types. Still a third student might have been so interested in looking at famous poems and thinking about how other characters in those poems might have responded to the speakers or to the main characters that she created a group of poems that showed this trait of response. In all cases, students would write a reflection about the collection of poems and how they demonstrated skills or traits appropriate to some of the qualities of those presented in the lessons. The teacher might give this collection a separate grade or might include this as part of the writing grade for the quarter. The evaluation would be centered on the completion of the work and on the written reflection, showing what the student learned or was able to accomplish. The student might even be asked, based on a rubric or traits developed prior to the end of the marking period, what grade he or she might assign to this collection.

My Own Evaluation System

My grading was based on the assumption that the work that students completed and handed in was the best they could do at that time. As a result, barring reasons for using other arrangements with students for modifications, my students were responsible for completing certain numbers: one thousand pages read in a quarter, ten literary letters, twenty pages in the writer's notebook, and six to seven finished, polished pieces of writing in their quarterly portfolio. If students did all of these things, they would get an A as a grade. Students had the option of showing how they took on more difficult tasks and were not able to satisfy the numbers requirement, and still earn the A grade. For example, the student might read the *Canterbury Tales* and two Shakespearean plays so that their numbers of pages read were not as many as other students but because of the difficulty, they could find the work to be equivalent. Another student might have written a twenty-page short story in addition to two other poems and therefore did not complete six finished pieces. He could argue that the work of the short story equates to several shorter pieces and that he too should receive full credit. In this way, students were allowed to negotiate their grade if they took a different road or chose a harder project. The point is to avoid punishing students who take risks, regardless of how successful they are in satisfying the numbers or turning out quality work. Their job was to demonstrate the things they've learned in the process and reflect on the process that led to success or failure. This is a very different way of evaluating student work. I found that students were very capable of working within this system and that they produced work in greater quantity and quality than they had ever done before in an assign-and-grade system.

The following is an example of Sheila's short reflection on a poem from the fourth quarter, "Day Ain't Long Enough." She did not choose to include this poem in her final portfolio but this reflection was one of a series that she submitted as part of the cover sheet for her fourth quarter portfolio.

> "Day Ain't Long Enough" . . . was written in the wee hours of the morning after a long, exhausting day at school. I thought, if only the day were twelve hours longer, I might be able to do all that needs to get done. . . . Hmm . . . , it led to poetry.

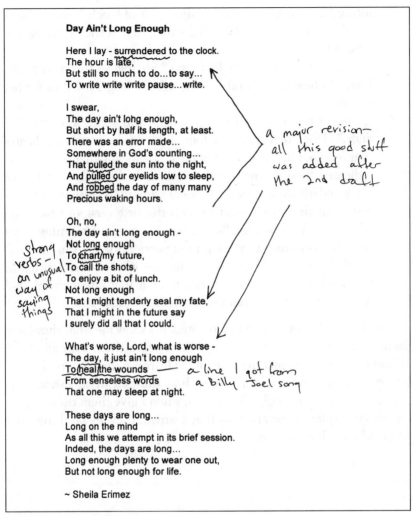

Figure 19–1 Sheila's Quarterly Portfolio Annotation

Included in this portfolio was a copy of the poem as well as Sheila's annotations, indicating some of the skills she demonstrated (see Figure 19–1). Here, she pointed out three skills or aspects of her learning and work as a writer.

1. "Strong verbs (infinitives)—an unusual way of saying things." Here Sheila is referring to three lines in her poem: "To chart my

future,/ To call the shots,/ To enjoy a bit of lunch." She is showing that she is aware of parallel structure and the power of specific action.

2. "A line I got from a Billy Joel song." She places this next to the line, "To heal the wounds" as she acknowledges a source for her writing.

3. "A major revision—All this good stuff was added after the 2nd draft." Here, Sheila points to four of the five stanzas and indicates that from her first draft she has made significant changes. She has indicated these changes with a yellow highlighter that I have since underlined and used a series of arrows. This annotation suggests that she wasn't satisfied with the first version, which she tells us had been written "in the wee hours of the morning," and that she continued to work on the poem until she was satisfied. Sheila has followed her instincts to trust what she has written in her notebook and then continue to craft that raw material, and she has shown this in her reflection and annotation.

I find it much more useful to have students show me what they have learned than make up tests to see if I can catch them with all of the things I've taught. Sometimes they show learning that occurred weeks and months ago and sometimes they show things learned a short time ago, even without my help. But always, when I give them these opportunities to explain what and how they learned, they reveal things that often take my breath away.

20

Holding a Poetry Reading

Friday Fever in Springtime

Imagine a Friday in May, perhaps the weekend before Memorial Day, and feel the growing excitement throughout the school building about the weekend plans. The atmosphere is electric. The feeling begins around second period, and you can sense it mounting with each passing period. Kids are calling to each other in the hallways and at their lockers about their plans for Friday night. By the later lunch periods, the glee is so thick you can almost touch it. By the last period, concentration on any subject matter is tough, and as students head for the busses or to their cars, there is almost a magnetic pull to get out into the May sun. Even those staying after school for sports or for the rare Friday club are in a holiday mood. You hear kids greeting teachers or fellow students, calling out, "Have a good weekend."

Now imagine that you've planned a schoolwide poetry reading for this day, one that students have heard about for weeks, one that they're looking forward to, one that they will attend during their English class so they can listen to their peers read their own poems, the poems of their friends, or poems they've come to love. It will be a day set aside just for them and it will be largely a senior-run day because they have been waiting for their turn since they first attended as ninth or tenth graders.

A few weeks beforehand, the English teachers meet to select the date and to go over some of the details including location and responsibilities. Two teachers volunteer to coordinate the whole day, including communicating with the administration, clearing the use of the location, and verifying the date with other school events. We have to choose between the library, which we've used from the beginning, and the auditorium, which is much bigger and has seating for all but isn't nearly as intimate. As auditoriums go, it is small and will only seat about four hundred people but it will seem cavernous for a poetry reading, especially at the beginning of the day and at those times when only one or two English classes might be scheduled. The disadvantage of the library is that we have to cart all of the chairs from the music wing and set them up and then, on Friday afternoon when everyone is looking to make a quick exit, we have to pull down all the chairs and return them to the music department. Most of the time, we go for the intimacy of the library and corral a few students to help us with the chairs and cleanup.

We speak to a handful of students about hosting the poetry reading. They will be the ones up front, greeting the students when they arrive, setting the ground rules, making sure of the order of things. We've also run poetry readings in which individual teachers are assigned to coordinate things during a specific period when their classes will be present. It works either way but it is a little more student-centered when it is orchestrated by them. If students are to be in charge, they need to decide what periods they will commit to the event and they will have to get permission from their teachers during those periods.

We spread the word to our classes, telling them of the date and the place of the poetry reading; the ground rules of respect for each other, themselves, their families, and their school; and we speak about appropriateness of language. We tell them that they can read poetry or prose, their own, a friend's, or work by a published author. I tell students who ask about extra credit that I don't believe in it and that a poetry reading is for its own enjoyment, not for a reward or punishment. People will read because they want to share something with others, not because they can gain some extra points for a class grade. Others disagree with me and offer extra credit.

English teacher Ginny Crispell captured some of the feelings that we experienced each year at the annual schoolwide poetry reading in her poem.

Poetry Reading: May 18
They are our own ideas, ideals, and fears,
    our past, our present, our hopes, and our dreams.
They come from the quarterback.

They come from the quiet girl
   who sits in the back row.
They come from those in black, heavy-metal T-shirts.
They come from the counter-culture kid
   whom we expect to have deep thoughts
   and outrageous opinions—he does.
They come to us set to music,
   played and sung with hidden talent.
They need to be heard; they need to be
   re-heard.
They are the poetry readings; they need to be.

                     —*V. Crispell*

Another Kind of Poetry Reading

My friend Bill Picchioni runs poetry readings at Lynbrook High School on Long Island, New York, but these are different because they are held at night and are attended on a voluntary basis. Bill explained how things work at his school.

"The evening goes something like this. First of all, there is a tradition of the readings, which goes back to the spring of 1986. This is a well-established event. So, when the school year begins, there are already the juniors and seniors who have been to six readings because we do three a year—fall, winter, and spring. A few of the sophomores are among the initiated and as the year goes on, several more become part of this event. One of the first questions continually asked of me in September is 'When is the first poetry reading?' Of course, the first reading is always two days before Thanksgiving. This way, alumni, most of whom are in college, can return and read as well.

"This past year, there were twenty-five alumni among the seventy or so students who attended. David Mahfouda, a former quarterback, lacrosse player, and valedictorian, flew down from Harvard for the day, read that night, and flew back for classes the next morning at 6 A.M.

"We have the readings on the auditorium stage. Several students bring candles. Many bake. Others bring store-bought cookies. I make sure there are enough cookies, snacks, juices, milk, and especially Mallomars for the break in the reading. Once the candles are lit and students and teachers are occupying the stage in a circle, sitting on the floor, sitting in chairs, arranging themselves in eagerness, we begin. I begin by welcoming everyone and especially thank the poets who have returned. Then I speak about the evening and how important the words will be to all of us sitting here. And I speak of how nonjudgmental this whole event is and how we can say what we really want to and not feel inhibited. But we must have respect for each other. We must listen, enjoy, appreciate. I tell them that this is an evening of spirit reading:

> When the spirit moves you, come up and read what you have. It may be your own work or the work of a friend or the work of a well-known writer. The important thing is that you want to share it with us.

"I usually begin by reading a few original pieces of my own. Then, I turn the evening over to them. Usually, there is a momentary hiatus as the whole idea sinks in. Here are seventy people rustling through their journals, books, scraps of paper, scribbling furiously until the precise moment when one student says, 'Okay, I'll start.' There is this great rush of relief because this is the opening of the floodgates. Once the first person reads, they start to crawl over each other to get up and read. Humor, anger, confusion, angst, joy, praise all flow from their pages. Then a guitar case opens up and Steven Green gives us a Dave Matthews song. This is followed by four students, Steven Cuevas, Amanda Rosenblum, Kevin Ferguson, and Gerry Ruotti, who do an a cappella rendition of "Seasons of Love" from *Rent*. Danny Fisher and Jessica Glazer stroll down to the piano and sing an original piece that they have been working on for this night. They are the heart and soul of their own youth. And for three hours they glow and bask in the praise and acceptance of their moment on stage. The quarterback next to the skateboarder next to the musician next to the barely-hanging-on student.

"When the night is over, I wait until everyone leaves as I clean up. A few stay behind to help and to prolong the magic of the evening. The energy is still so high that it is difficult to go home right away. When I do get home, my wife's first question is always, 'How did it go?' Invariably I say, 'You're not going to believe this, but it was the most incredible reading we've ever had.'

"The first question asked the next day in school is 'When is the next poetry reading?'"

150

Bill sent me a short email about the latest poetry reading:

Had a poetry reading at school just before Thanksgiving. 150 students showed. Spilled down over the risers and out into the seats of the auditorium. Guitars, drums, singers, poets, teachers, administrators packed in perfect respect of the word and of each other. Blew my mind—and everyone else's.

What I conclude from Bill's experiences and from our own is that if you want to legitimize poetry in the classroom, you need to allow it to happen in public readings, be they during school days with the whole student body or in smaller, voluntary groups at night. When students can participate freely and express their thoughts and hear others doing it, they are more willing to work hard at the craft in the classroom.

21

Appearing in Print

Mesmerized Students

At 7:30 in the morning, on this last day of school in late June, the temperature is climbing and the humidity is thick and heavy. The residue of stale, hot air slows students as they move to their homerooms to pick up their report cards, pay lost book fines, return to their busses, and head home for the summer. "One hour, that's it; then we're outta here." But not these years. This has become a very literate environment, this high school with its poetry readings, staggering increases in the circulation of library books, successful entries into writing contests. These are different times.

And just like that, in swoops a student carrying copies of the final edition of the school newspaper, a copy for each student. However, not far behind this staff member come two students pushing a cart piled high with copies of *Entre Nous*, the literary magazine to which I am currently the advisor. As quickly as the newspapers were soaked up, so the literary magazines are received because in a school of approximately 950 students, there will be at least 250 students whose work will be included. For the next thirty minutes, you can walk into just about every one of thirty classrooms in the building and see students reading silently or talking quietly about a piece they have spotted. Perhaps it is one they have written, perhaps it was written by a friend, perhaps even the piece is written about someone they know.

When the students have received their report cards and have been dismissed to the busses, there are very few copies of *Entre Nous* that have been left on the desks the way newspapers are often left on airport waiting room seats. If you could catch up to some students and ask about the literary magazine, they would tell you that they planned to keep their copies because of some of the writing in it or perhaps to show it to someone at home. There is no doubt that the literary magazine is held in high esteem by most students.

Sponsoring a Literary Magazine

When I was in high school, I would have been the last person anyone would have thought of as a sponsor of a literary magazine. I don't recall there being a literary magazine nor were there any opportunities in classes or elsewhere to write for an audience of fellow students other than the school newspaper. Throughout my teaching career, literary magazines seemed to showcase the work of a few of the finest student writers. I never understood where exactly this writing got done, at home or after school in the small literary magazine office where the elite few hung out. So when the principal came to me in 1989 and asked me to convince any department member to take over as advisor of the literary magazine, I was faced with an almost impossible task. No one seemed to want the job, though the pay was not the obstacle. The reasons were the time commitment, the difficulty of getting students to submit work, and not knowing anything about the process.

At the same time, I had been editor of the district newsletter for the past two years and we had used an outside agency to take my typed copy and turn it into a newsletter, using desktop publishing equipment and software. But that same year through a grant, a Macintosh computer, a laser printer, and a scanner arrived in my office for my use in producing the newsletter. Jerry and I set to work to learn how to use all of this equipment for our classes. We went to a desktop publishing class to learn how to use paging software, to scan texts, and to do many other dazzling tasks. By October of that year, we were making overhead transparencies of our students' work, we were creating layouts with boxes and shadings and other fancy things, and we were allowing students to take turns using the computer during class to type their own work. I suddenly saw how the literary magazine could be similar to the newsletter: students were learning about layouts, were typing and collecting their work in files, and collaborating with others to share and produce their work.

It was then that I decided that if I couldn't get another teacher to take over the literary magazine, I would do so myself. After all, I had plenty of student work to draw from since Jerry and I had converted all of our classes to workshop environments and students were turning out amazing amounts of quality work—poems, short stories, personal experience narratives, dialogues, essays, literary letters, reflections, and more. So I came at the magazine from a different perspective; instead of creating a literary magazine and asking students to contribute so it could be published, I saw all of this work in its development stages that could be presented and enjoyed by peers and parents in a published form. I gathered a small staff of students and we met every Friday after school from December until late May when we sent the magazine to the printer. Our idea was not to gather the work of the elite writers but to allow all students, regardless of their academic status, to have their work appear in publication, a collection of treasured writings rather than writing treasures.

At the end of the school year, students and teachers find pleasure in looking back at the diverse works produced in all of the various classes and grades. Thus, the literary magazine serves as a summing up of the writing accomplished that school year. The magazine is the visible evidence of those efforts.

Using the Literary Magazine as a Teaching Tool

As the advisor, I made sure that we ordered about two hundred extra copies. Some we sent to administrators and people in other buildings in the district but we kept the majority of the copies in my office to be used by English teachers during the following year. I kept a stack in each room that I taught in and would frequently pass out copies to show a particular work or just to allow students to examine writing from the previous year. These would often serves as inspiration for topics for students to write about or as models for how the work might look. Once again, showing the work of a student who might still be in the school allowed for reinforcement of that writer and expanded the community of writers as other students mentioned seeing his or her work in class. In a short time, the idea of students writing for other students became an accepted practice and the school culture began to be transformed.

154

One thing I avoided was submitting the magazine for prizes, awards, and recognition. I felt that the students who helped assemble the magazine had no knowledge of such awards and that winning had little effect on their lives. I felt that the only one to benefit would be me and I didn't think it was worth the time and effort to fill out the forms. The magazine was for students, not for me.

Writing Contests

Contrary to my seeking awards for the literary magazine, I encouraged students to submit their work to various writing contests. In other schools or in other times, we might have announced to our students a particular contest and urged some to write and submit their work. Most students would realize that they had very little chance of winning and that they already had too much schoolwork to do. Besides, this didn't really count as English work and students would still have to do the regular work for English class. This seemed more like a burden without much upside to it. However, as I began to see all of the work that students were doing, and I looked at what these contests were asking writers to do, I realized that most of the work was already done. It remained for students to make some adjustments in length or format and for us to send it off and wait. We were amazed at how many students won recognition for their writing and without being required to do much extra work on their part. As a result of these awards, we began to set aside a special section in the literary magazine to group these works by students. Sometimes we put this in the center pages and sometimes at the end, usually designated by a different color paper.

One Particular Contest

Generally, we didn't believe in assigning a particular contest for all students to enter but we made one exception. Each year, the Walt Whitman Birthplace Society ran a contest for students from the primary grades to high school. The purpose of the contest was to familiarize students with Walt Whitman, who was born and lived on Long Island in a town not too far from us. Each year, the committee would select a different trait found in Whitman's poetry, find a poem exemplifying it, and ask students to use that trait in a poem for the contest.

Usually contests require the school to screen the entries and send only four or five submissions. The nice thing about the Walt Whitman poetry contest was that the committee accepted entries from all students. We submitted poems from all of our students because we thought our students would benefit from imitating or applying a trait of Whitman's and using it in their own poem about Long Island, one of the requirements of the contest. In addition, there was a second category called a class anthology. Since Jerry and I had all of the students in each of our classes write Whitman poems, we simply took these poems and arranged them in a publication using our paging software. Very often, we had a student teacher and we would ask him or her to sponsor or work with a particular class to put together that anthology. Students would sometimes bring in small pictures that might go on the same page as their poem. As students on the literary magazine staff began to grow in number and experience with the paging software, they often took on the same responsibility that a student teacher would and they became the editors for a particular class anthology. The results each year were the same: we swept the fields in the age groups of our students. If sixty prizes were given out for grades two through twelve, we would have at least twenty of those winners. The director of the society used to kid us each year on the annual awards Sunday as we arrived with some of our students, saying that they had changed the judges or they had changed the rules, trying to keep us from winning so many of the prizes but that they had failed again.

I always understood the issue. In a way, it wasn't fair. We were reading and writing poetry all year and our students were living and breathing it. Students in other schools were only doing it for brief periods of time and so our students seemed to have a great advantage. Even as they wrote to us from college, they reflected on their ease with poetry as they looked at the struggles and fears of their roommates and friends who seemed to be so intimidated by it all. Our students had been feasting on these meals from the start and were well nourished with this food for the soul.

Epilogue

On Caring

The horse doesn't care what you [the trainer or jockey]
know until he knows that you care.

At a recent workshop with teachers, I started by asking them to do several quick writes, including one that began with the prompt, "My students know I care because. . . ." A recent article in *Educational Leadership,* an ASCD journal, in an issue focusing on caring schools and communities, pointed out the misrepresentation of the term *caring,* showing that students don't necessarily think teachers care because they are easy or give them all sorts of breaks, or have comfortable rooms, or even give them candies and other goodies. Students say that teachers care if they listen to them, allow their ideas to be treated with respect, allow them to take on challenges, and give them honest feedback.

At the heart of the stories and procedures we've told is our bottom-line belief that we start first with caring, by giving our students their voice. Doing so, paradoxically, heaps blessings of all sorts on us. One summer I wrote twenty-five poems, one in response to each eleventh-grade student whose portfolio I had taken home to read during the quiet of summer days. Just before returning to school in September, I wrote in the second person to Stephanie Sulc, describing not only the beauty of the portfolio arrangement but how the writings continued to take me on a journey to other places, as well as into the mind and soul of the writer.

Golden Splash
In early September,
I am overcome with another new horizon
that forms with each mist

that burns off the gold of the sun.
Every page is a new day,
perfect, and yet different from the last one.
I am caught up by it all
and do not care at the moment
to move on
into the next school year
and away from my horizon of the past.

I am with you and the endless empty pages
of your shiny writer's notebook
of a year ago,
and I am frozen with you on the icy field hockey bench,
or on your grandpa's knee years ago,
or behind the masks we all wear.
I am visiting a teacher with you
or cruisin' down 347 in Kerry's car.

These are the days I will remember
because you've reminded me
with your words
of how blessed and lucky I am.

When I finished all twenty-five poems, I wrote a final one.

Portfolio Poems
Who ever heard of it but there they are,
25 poems
about portfolios.
If you asked me in June,
I'd have said you were crazy
but I did it,
a poem
for
every
student
not great poems, maybe,
nothing too profound,
but a tribute, nevertheless,
for the emotions they provided

on hot summer days,
on June nights of back pain,
of August mornings
on the porch of an inn at Hampton Beach,
and for the times
they moved me
in ways the writer
will never know.
These poems,
meager as the are,
give thanks
for the riches
of a blessed
and lucky teacher.

So, if you have reached this final page and have a question or a comment that you care to make, you can send an email to Campyhits@aol.com. My hero, Robert Cormier, included his phone number in *I Am the Cheese,* allowing readers to call him. I could do no less in responding to an email, just to show I care too.

Works Cited

Atwell, Nancie. 1987. *In the Middle: Writing, Reading, and Learning with Adolescents*. Portsmouth, NH: Heinemann.

———. 1992. Talk given at the NCTE conference, Louisville, KY, November.

———. 1995. Talk given at the NCTE conference, San Diego, CA, November.

———. 1998. *In the Middle: New Understandings About Writing, Reading, and Learning*. 2d ed. Portsmouth, NH: Heinemann.

Barfield, Owen. 1984. *Poetic Diction: A Study in Meaning*. Middletown, CT: Wesleyan University Press.

Beers, Kylene. 2003. *When Kids Can't Read, What Teachers Can Do*. Portsmouth, NH: Heinemann.

Bly, Robert. 1983. "The Six Powers of Poetry" (audiotape). Big Sur, CA: Dolphin Tapes.

Bruchac, Joseph, and Michael J. Caduto. 1995. *Keepers of the Animals: Native American Stories and Wildlife Activities for Children*. Golden, CO: Fulcrum.

Calkins, Lucy. 1992. Talk given at the NCTE conference, Louisville, KY, November.

Collins, Billy. 2003. *Poetry 180: A Turning Back to Poetry*. New York: Random House.

Daniels, Harvey. 1994. *Literature Circles: Voice and Choice in the Student-Centered Classroom*. York, ME: Stenhouse.

———. 2002. *Literature Circles: Voice and Choice in Book Clubs and Reading Groups*. York, ME: Stenhouse.

Dean, Sandra. 2003. In *Teaching with Fire: Poetry That Sustains the Courage to Teach*, edited by Sam M. Intrator and Megan Scribner, 24. San Francisco: Jossey-Bass.

Dias, Patrick. 1987. *Making Sense of Poetry: Patterns in the Process*. Winnipeg, MB: Canadian Council of Teachers of English.

Dillard, Annie. 1974. *Pilgrim at Tinker Creek*. New York: Harper & Row.

Ferlinghetti, Lawrence. 1958. "Autobiography." In *Coney Island of the Mind*. San Francisco: City Lights Press.

Fletcher, Ralph. 1996. *A Writer's Notebook: Unlocking the Writer Within You*. New York: Avon.

Heard, Georgia. 1999a. *Awakening the Heart: Exploring Poetry in Elementary and Middle School*. Portsmouth, NH: Heinemann.

———. 1999b. Talk given at the NCTE conference, Denver, CO, November.

Intrator, Sam M., and Megan Scribner, eds. 2003. *Teaching with Fire: Poetry That Sustains the Courage to Teach*. San Francisco: Jossey-Bass.

Jaccarino, Victor. 1996. Personal communication.

Lee, Harper. 1960. *To Kill a Mockingbird*. New York: J. B. Lippincott.

Lee, Li-Young. 2001. *Book of My Nights*. Rochester, NY: BOA Editions.

Mahoney, Jim. 2002. *Power and Portfolios*. Portsmouth, NH: Heinemann.

Murdoch, Iris. 1992. *Metaphysics as a Guide to Morals*. New York: Penguin.

Murray, Donald. 2004. *A Writer Teaches Writing*. Revised 2d ed. Boston: Heinle.

Nesbit, Edith. 2003. In *Teaching with Fire: Poetry That Sustains the Courage to Teach*, edited by Sam M. Intrator and Megan Scribner. San Francisco: Jossey-Bass.

Olds, Sharon. 1992. "The Present Moment." In *The Father*. New York: Alfred A. Knopf.

Rief, Linda. 2003. Talk given at the NCTE conference, San Francisco, November 22.

Romano, Tom. 1995. *Writing with Passion*. Portsmouth, NH: Heinemann.

Salinger, J. D. 1953. *The Catcher in the Rye*. New York: Bantam.

Smith, Michael, and Jeffrey Wilhem. 2002. *"Reading Don't Fix No Chevys": Literacy in the Lives of Young Men*. Portsmouth, NH: Heinemann.

Tsujimoto, Joseph I. 1996. *Teaching Poetry Writing to Adolescents.* Urbana, IL: National Council of Teachers of English.

Whitman, Walt. 1982. *Complete Poetry and Collected Prose.* New York: Library of America.

Wilhelm, Jeffrey. 2004. *Reading Is Seeing.* New York: Scholastic.

Index of Authors and Works

Writers/Poets

Works